Differentiatin Assessment in Middle and High School English and Social Studies

Sheryn Spencer Waterman

EYE ON EDUCATION
6 DEPOT WAY WEST, SUITE 106
LARCHMONT, NY 10538
(914) 833–0551
(914) 833–0761 fax
www.eyeoneducation.com

Library of Congress Cataloging-in-Publication Data

Waterman, Sheryn Northey.
Differentiating assessment in middle and high school English and social studies / by Sheryn Waterman.
    p. cm.
    ISBN 978-1-59667-111-9
    1. High school students—Rating of—United States. 2. Middle school students—Rating of—United States. 3. High schools—United States—Examinations—Language arts. 4. Middle schools—United States—Examinations—Language arts. 5. High schools—United States—Examinations—Social sciences. 6. Middle schools—United States—Examinations—Social sciences. I. Title.
    LB3060.26.W38 2008
    373.126—dc22

                                                        2008046886

10 9 8 7 6 5 4 3 2 1

Also Available from EYE ON EDUCATION

**Differentiating Assessment in
Middle and High School Mathematics and Science**
Sheryn Spencer Waterman

**Handbook on Differentiated Instruction
for Middle and High Schools**
Sheryn Spencer Northey

Formative Assessment: Responding to Your Students
Harry Grover Tuttle

Differentiated Assessment for Middle and High School Classrooms
Deborah Blaz

**Teacher-Made Assessments:
Connecting Curriculum, Instruction, and Student Learning**
Christopher R. Gareis and Leslie W. Grant

**Short Cycle Assessment:
Improving Student Achievement Through Formative Assessment**
Susan Lang, Todd Stanley and Betsy Moore

**Formative Assessment for English Language Arts:
A Guide for Middle and High School Teachers**
Amy Benjamin

**Performance-Based Learning and Assessment
in Middle School Science**
K. Michael Hibbard

**Assessment in Middle and High School Mathematics:
A Teacher's Guide**
Daniel Brahier

**A Collection of Performance Tasks and Rubrics:
Primary School Mathematics**
Charlotte Danielson and Pia Hansen Powell

Upper Elementary School Mathematics
Charlotte Danielson

Middle School Mathematics
Charlotte Danielson

High School Mathematics
Charlotte Danielson and Elizabeth Marquez

Meet the Author

Sheryn Spencer Waterman is an educational consultant and coach who specializes in curriculum design, differentiation, assessment, and literacy. Her many accomplishments include "Teacher of the Year" in two schools, National Board Certification (renewed in 2007), Founding Fellow for the Teacher's Network Leadership Institute, and founding interim President of the North Carolina Association of Literacy Coaches. She came to the field of education after a career as a psychotherapist and consultant. She has worked on many local, state, regional, and national projects to promote quality teaching. She is also a doctoral student at the University of North Carolina at Greensboro.

When she was known as Sheryn Spencer Northey, she wrote the highly successful *Handbook on Differentiated Instruction for Middle and High Schools.*

Free Downloads

Many of the examples discussed and displayed in this book are can be downloaded and printed out by anyone who has purchased this book. Book buyers have permission to download and print out these Adobe Acrobat documents.

You can access these downloads by visiting Eye On Education's Web site: www.eyeoneducation.com. Click on FREE Downloads. Or search or browse our Web site from our homepage to find this book and then scroll down for downloading instructions.

You'll need your book-buyer access code: **WAE-7107–2**

Index of Downloads

TABLE OF CONTENTS

1

Differentiated Assessment

Introduction

Assessment is probably the most important aspect of the learning experience. In fact, I suggest generally that the ratio of instruction to assessment should be approximately 1 to 4. For example, for every 10 minutes of instruction, the teacher should consider including approximately 40 minutes of assessment. More than allowing teachers and students to know what students already know and what they are learning or have learned, assessment supports instruction so that learning can take place.

In addition to being critically important to instruction, assessments that address students' needs are the most useful. Focusing on how teachers might differentiate assessment should greatly improve learning outcomes. This book provides an overview of assessment in conjunction with differentiation, an explanation of general differentiated assessment strategies, three chapters of examples differentiated by readiness for at-risk, average, and gifted or highly advanced students, and a chapter that shows how to put several assessment strategies together in a differentiated unit of study.

Some Concepts to Understand

There are many important issues to consider as we explore differentiated assessment. First, we should define the important terms that help us understand how learning, assessment, and evaluation interact. Figure 1.1 is an interesting visual adapted from Trussell-Cullen (1998, p. 7).

Figure 1.1. Learning→Assessment→Evaluation Loop→Learning, etc.

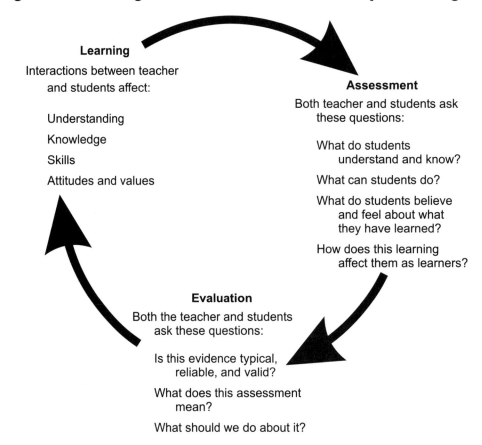

Learning

Interactions between teacher
and students affect:

Understanding

Knowledge

Skills

Attitudes and values

Assessment

Both teacher and students ask
these questions:

What do students
understand and know?

What can students do?

What do students believe
and feel about what
they have learned?

How does this learning
affect them as learners?

Evaluation

Both the teacher and students
ask these questions:

Is this evidence typical,
reliable, and valid?

What does this assessment
mean?

What should we do about it?

Defining Differentiated Assessment

Keeping these distinctions in mind, this book will focus on the "assessment" part of these concepts. We define "differentiation" as adjustments teachers make to address the learning needs of all students. (Northey, 2005; Tomlinson, 1995, 1999, 2003; Wormeli, 2006) When we combine assessment with differentiation, we can say that "differentiated assessment" is the process of finding out in a fair way what each individual student knows, understands, and can do (KUD), how they feel about what they have learned, and how they feel about themselves as learners.

Here is a list of criteria for good assessments suggested by Rick Wormeli (2006, pp. 39–41; see his book for a full discussion of each one).

Good assessment

♦ Increases learning rather than merely documenting it

♦ Chooses what is most important for students to learn

♦ Helps inform instruction

♦ Goes on throughout the unit of study and never saved for only "the end"

- Addresses knowledge, understanding, and skill development in a meaningful way

- Is authentic either to a real-world experience or to the way the information was taught

- Shows clear and valid information about what students have actually learned

- Is reliable across time and across classes of students

- Is timed well to check for learning

- Is integrated with other subjects

- Requires use of a variety of tools

- Helps teachers determine students' misunderstanding of the what students are learning

- Asks for students' input

- Is varied and differentiated

If teachers want to become skilled at implementing differentiated assessment in their classrooms, they might address these six parts of assessment planning as follows in Figure 1.2.

Figure 1.2. Six Parts of Planning Differentiated Assessment

1. **Students' needs:**	Who are the students in terms of: (a) readiness, (b) interests, and (c) learning and thinking styles, and what do they already know about the topic?
2. **Curriculum:**	What enduring essential knowledge (EEK) (expressed as essential questions [EQ]) do these students need to know, understand, and do (KUD)? Note that the measurable objective(s) is listed separately in Part 3 below but is also included in the curriculum.
3. **Measurable objectives:**	How will the teacher measure that learning?
4. **Differentiation:**	How should the teacher differentiate the assessment to meet students' learning needs?
5. **Procedures:**	What procedures will the teacher follow to implement the assessment?
6. **Assessment audit:**	How will teachers evaluate the alignment of the assessment(s) and procedures so that they have a clear picture of what each student knows, understands, and can do related to the content?

Students' Needs

In the first step of this implementation process, the teacher should assess students' readiness, interests, and learning or thinking styles. The following sections are an overview of how we should think about these factors.

Readiness

Assessment and the Zone of Proximal Development

When teachers plan assessments for students, they need to make certain to align them with students' readiness to learn. If the assessment is too simple or not sensitive to the students' level of development, then students may feel less motivated to stretch toward higher levels of learning. Teachers should be aware of what Vygotsky (1978) calls the "zone of proximal development" (ZPD), which is defined as the difference between what a person can do alone and what the person needs help to do. Most teachers know early in the year how well their students read, how well they solve learning problems, and how motivated they are to learn. If the teacher needs specific tools to assess these issues, Northey (2005) has several ideas for assessing reading, interests, and learning styles. Teachers must also at times use materials above or below the readiness level of some or all of their students. Picture books on the lower end and computer-generated explanations on the upper end can be excellent resources for differentiating content, but teachers need to make sure students do not feel demeaned or frustrated by these resources. Teachers also need to make sure to constantly inspire students to learn at higher and higher levels. Assessments that pay attention to the ZPD stretch students toward greater depth of knowledge and independence as learners. Teachers need to make sure to challenge students toward their highest capacity without overwhelming them. This balance within the ZPD is the key to successful differentiated assessment.

Interests

Teachers should take time to learn students' interests and emotional investment in their subject area (e.g., math, English) as well as individual units of study (e.g., decimals, plot of a story). As we know, motivation plays an important role in students' achievement. The teacher may use interests on certain areas to leverage student engagement in less interesting, but necessary, topics of learning. For example, a teacher who knows her students are interested in basketball can use basketball themes to teach difficult math or English concepts.

Learning and Thinking Styles

Teachers should find and administer surveys to determine students' learning styles. It is important that teachers keep in mind that learning and thinking styles are not static and that they can change based on the topic. Figure 1.3 is a short chart of some of the most popular learning and thinking styles.

Figure 1.3. Popular Learning and Thinking Styles

Number grouped by	Name of Inventory and Where to Find It
Three	1. Kinesthetic, Visual, or Auditory—Learning Channels: Preference checklist from Lynn O'Brien, (1990)
	2. Creative, Analytical, or Practical—Thinking Styles from Richard Sternberg (1997)
Four	1. Imaginative, Investigative, Realistic, or Analytical— What Kind of Fruit are You? from Kathleen Butler (1987)
	2. Mastery, Interpersonal, Understanding, and Self-Expressive—Silver, Strong, and Perini (2007)
	3. Visual, Auditory, Kinesthetic, and Tactual—Rita and Kenneth Dunn (1993)
Five or more	1. Narrative, Logical, Foundational, Aesthetic, or Experiential—Entry Points for learning Howard Gardner (1993)
	2. Verbal/Linguistic, Logical/Mathematical, Spatial, Bodily Kinesthetic, Musical, Interpersonal, Intrapersonal, Naturalist—the Multiple Intelligences Checklist—Howard Gardner (1993)
See http://eliot.needham.k12.ma.us/technology/di2/styles.htm for an exceptional overview of learning styles.	

At the beginning of Chapters 3, 4, and 5, teachers will find a detailed explanation of students' readiness levels as follows: at risk, average, and gifted or highly advanced. Chapter 3 is leveled for at-risk students; Chapter 4 is leveled for average students; and Chapter 5 is leveled for gifted or highly advanced students. Within each chapter teachers will find a description of special factors and issues related to readiness grouping. Each strategy also addresses students' interests and learning and thinking styles.

Curriculum

If teachers plan to differentiate assessment, they must have a working understanding of the major aspects of curriculum planning. It is critical that teachers determine meaningful curriculum goals that address students' needs in the context of mandated curriculum standards. If teachers do not use some method of clearly determining the direction for learning, they will not be able to assess effectively. When most teachers sign their teaching contracts, they agree to teach some form of determined curriculum, such as a standard course of study (SCOS). All assessment plans should flow from this. Figure 1.4 offers a brief explanation of some helpful concepts for teachers to plan useful assessment goals.

Figure 1.4. Parts of Curriculum

Title	Abbreviation	Explanation
Standard course of study	SCOS	Most states have curriculum standards that teachers are required to address. These standards may have goals and objectives that teachers can easily incorporate into their unit plans. Often they need to be "unpacked" or analyzed (pulled apart) so that the teacher can determine how to translate these standards for student learning.
Essential enduring knowledge (also know as: big idea, enduring understanding, etc.; here we call it "understanding.")	EEK	The EEK represents the core of the unit of study. It is what teachers wants their students to remember from a unit of study for the rest of their lives (enduring). Having a well-conceptualized EEK is critical to planning differentiated assessments. When teachers are dealing with students who may need more time to learn, the EEK can help that teacher concentrate on ideas that have high priority so that no one will waste critical learning time on less important aspects of the topic or concept.
Essential questions	EQs	Essential questions make the unit topic relevant through the inquiry that is embedded in the notion of learning. Students might ask these questions with teacher help, or the teacher might pose them with student approval. Skills, knowledge, understanding, and objectives must answer these questions.
Knowledge, understanding, and can do	KUDs	In unit planning, this is a thorough and accurate list of the things students will know, understand, and be able to do as a result of the learning activities. Differentiated assessment is impossible to design without a clear idea of all the things students need to know, understand, and do.
Measurable objectives	MOs	The teachers' objectives must be measurable and must answer the EQs. To write a measurable objective, teachers must think about moving up a taxonomy of thinking skills for the thinking verb part of the objective (e.g., students will generate, create, apply, etc.). They should also write the product, response criterion or criteria, and content to write a comprehensive measurable objective.

In Chapters 3 through 5, as a way of introducing each assessment strategy, teachers will note a chart that provides an overview of curriculum goals. An example of the standard course of study is omitted because each district or state will have its own language. The chart looks like Figure 1.5.

Figure 1.5. Curriculum

SCOS	Essential Question (EQ)	Know	Understand	Do

Note: For the purpose of clarity, the EEK is incorporated within the EQs and KUDs and Curriculum Goals is shortened to Curriculum. *Also, the Measurable Objective(s) (MOs), although addressed separately, should be part of the Curriculum.*

Measurable Objectives

In Figure 1.2, part 3 of major differentiated assessment strategies includes a suggested measurable objective or objectives. This objective includes the following parts:

♦ An introductory phrase: "Students will or students will be able to…"

♦ A defining thinking verb from "New Bloom," for example, thinking verbs range in thinking skills from "recalling" to "producing"

♦ A product, for example, ranging in complexity from "a list" to "an invention"

♦ A statement about a specific quantitative or qualitative criterion for a sufficient response (Teachers can note responses that go above and beyond the standards they set at the beginning of the unit.)

♦ Specified content the teacher will assess

The generic template is shown in Figure 1.6.

Figure 1.6. Measurable Objective Template

Introduction	Thinking Verb	Product	Response Criterion	Content
For example: Students will…	recall	in order to list	at least five important facts	that define plant and animal cells.

Differentiation

When teachers know the students' needs in Figure 1.2, part 1, they will be able to address those needs in terms of a differentiation plan.

Teachers will see this chart as follows (Figure 1.7).

Figure 1.7. Differentiation Plan

Readiness—	Interests—	Learning styles—
students' or the classes' level of ability or capacity to be successful independently or with help on any given learning task	students' or the classes' naturally found interests that inspire them to learn any given task	students' best or favorite mode of learning on any given task (Noting that the preferred style may shift given the task)

Procedures

For each major differentiation assessment strategy, teachers will see a detailed list of steps they might take to implement it. They will also find specific and general examples to help them duplicate the idea or adapt it to meet their specific needs.

Assessment Audit

Each teacher needs to conduct an audit of the assessment strategy with his or her own students. Figure 1.8 is a useful template to check for assessment alignment. Figure 1.9 shows the Differentiating Assessment: Six-Part Template.

Figure 1.8. Differentiated Assessment Audit*

1. How did the assessment of students' needs match the assessment strategy or strategies for the unit of study? Was anyone left out? Why? How?

2. How did assessment strategy or strategies match the curriculum goals for the unit of study?

3. How were the needs of every child represented in each differentiated assessment strategy or strategies?

4. How did the measurable objective show best evidence of student achievement for the lesson or unit of study?

5. How did the assessment strategy or strategies match content?

6. How did this assessment strategy or strategies work overall:

   | 1 | 2 | 3 | 4 | 5 |

   (Circle 1 = low and 5 = high)

*Teachers can conduct an audit for each strategy or for the strategies they used to assess a unit of study.

Figure 1.9. Differentiating Assessment: Six-Part Template

1. Students' Needs (described in detail)				
2. Curriculum				
SCOS	Essential Question (EQ)	Know	Understand	Do (See MO below)
3. Measurable Objectives				
Introduction	Thinking Verb(s)	Product	Response Criterion	Content
4. Differentiation				
Readiness		Interests		Learning Styles
5. Assessment Procedures—Listed by steps				
6. Assessment Audit (see above)				

Concepts Critical to
Effective Differentiated Assessments

Focus on Competence—Revision Mentality

Assessment strategies will differ based on the philosophical approach a teacher takes toward teaching and learning; however, regardless of what the teacher believes, it is important that the focus of instruction is on students gaining competence rather than teachers covering material so that they can issue a grade. With any perspective, the bottom line needs to be that the work is not finished until it is the best a student can do. For formative assessments, it is critical that teachers allow students to learn from their mistakes and to revise if what they have produced is substandard. The student might be the judge of when the work is finished rather than the teacher. From this perspective the revision process becomes an important and necessary step in the learning process. If a student completes a task perfectly every time, then the teacher may wonder if the assessment is truly challenging. Instead of giving a student an "F" as feedback on his or her work, the teacher might give the feedback as "Not yet." These two words are far more encouraging than and "F" for "Failure."

Assessment and Motivation

The best method of motivating learning is using assessment to help students feel they are successfully learning. Brain-based and cognitive researchers have been promoting the idea for some time now that the brain seeks complexity and wants to learn. Some teachers fail to realize the motivational impact of assessment in motivation. They might spend inordinate time and energy designing elaborate reward systems when they could get even more student motivation from cleverly designed assessments.

Time, the Learning Gap, and a Viable Curriculum

It is important that teachers make sure they have enough time to assess the most important knowledge and concepts for all students because the gap between those who are educated and those who struggle gets ever wider if instructional practices do not address the needs of all students. Also according to research (Marzano, 2003) many state-mandated curricula are not viable in allowing adequate time for all students to demonstrate mastery of their goals and objectives; therefore, teachers must prioritize those that might be most meaningful for their students' survival and well-being in their communities. If teachers take the time all students need for mastery rather than letting pacing guides rush them into coverage, they may actually save the time they might need for reteaching. Wiggins' & McTighe's (1998) "Three Circle Audit" is a great tool to help teachers determine their priorities. The critical idea to keep in mind is "What do you think your students should remember about this topic for the rest of their lives?" That is what you focus your assessment efforts on.

Differentiating Assessment in the Twenty-First Century

Differentiated assessment is important as we ask our students to develop twenty-first century skills. Students need to learn facts that are critical to their content area, but they need to learn them in the context of solving academic or real-world problems. Too many teachers plan assessments that determine if students have recalled facts related to their content areas, and they seem to be convinced that students must continue to recall facts, or they will not pass the test or be prepared for the next grade level. Most assessments of learning have moved beyond this low level of thinking. Teachers need to understand that they are short-changing their students by taking too much of the precious learning time to find out if students remember these facts isolated from problem solving. They need to *prioritize* teaching students how to learn facts as they analyze, apply, create, and evaluate them to solve problems.

We must adjust our thinking about standard forms of assessment, such as multiple choice tests or short answer tests of factual knowledge. By doing this we make room and time for a new level of competence. Within the information age, we realize that students no longer need to learn a set of facts that will help them succeed in a simple society. Our society is now highly complex and global. Teachers need to begin designing assessments that address the demands of the twenty-first century. As we look at differentiated assessment, we need to keep in mind that we need to assess students' abilities (Figure 1.10).

Figure 1.10. Twenty-First Century Skills

Digital Age Literacy	**Basic, Scientific, and Technological Literacy**
	◆ Read critically
	◆ Write persuasively
	◆ Think logically
	◆ Solve complex problems in science and mathematics
	Visual and Information Literacy
	◆ Use visualization skills to decipher, interpret, note patterns, and communicate using imagery
	◆ Assess information efficiently and effectively
	◆ Evaluate information critically and completely
	◆ Use information accurately and creatively
	Cultural Literacy and Global Awareness
	◆ Know, understand, and appreciate other cultures
	◆ Know, understand, and appreciate virtual realities.
Inventive Thinking and Intellectual Capital	**Adaptability, Managing Complexity, and Self-Direction**
	◆ React independently to changing conditions
	◆ Self-direct learning
	◆ Analyze new conditions as they arise
	◆ Identify new skills to deal with new conditions
	◆ Independently make a plan to respond to new conditions
	◆ Take contingencies into account
	◆ Anticipate changes
	◆ Understand how systems are interconnected.
	Curiosity, Creativity, and Risk Taking
	◆ Adjust and adapt to changing situations
	◆ Exercise curiosity and creativity
	Higher-Order Thinking and Sound Reasoning
	◆ Plan, design, execute, and evaluate problems using technological tools

Interactive Communication—Social and Personal Skills	**Teaming and Collaboration**
	♦ Work in teams to accomplish complex tasks
	♦ Use technology to provide virtual workplaces for more timely and repetitive collaborations
	Personal and Social Responsibility
	♦ Accept responsibility for ethical value judgments that guide the application of science and technology in society
	Interactive Communication
	♦ Understand how to use technological communications
	♦ Know the etiquette of various technological environments
Quality, State of the Arts, Results	**Prioritizing, Planning, and Managing Results**
	♦ Demonstrate flexibility and creativity to anticipate unexpected outcomes of planning, managing, and anticipating contingencies related to project goal setting
	Effective Use of Real World Tools
	♦ Use digital tools to help people solve problems for themselves
	♦ Choosing the appropriate tools for a task and applying them to real world situations to promote creativity, construction of models, preparation of publications, and other creative works
	♦ Focus on "know how" and "know who" rather than just "know what" as most important information
	High-Quality Results with Real-World Application
	♦ Build authentic products with a variety of tools
	♦ Develop deep insights concerning whatever tools are used

"Twenty-First Century Skills," retrieved November 25, 2007 at http://www.ncrel.org/sdrs/.

As we design differentiated assessments, we need to keep these twenty-first century skills in mind. We also need to constantly remind ourselves that the purpose of anything we teach our students results in their growth toward academic, social, and emotional competence. Here are some core skills teachers should remember to make sure they are including in differentiated assessments of students' work.

♦ *Reading* not just for understanding but for evaluating

♦ *Writing* to persuade

♦ *Thinking* logically at high levels to solve problems in our complex world

♦ *Using technology* to access information and to solve problems

What Is Developmentally Appropriate in Zeros and Make-Up Work?

When teachers think of assessing students to help prepare them for college and/or the world of work in the twenty-first century, they need to remember that students may only care about the present. Most students cannot conceive of themselves as potential adults in the real world or care about how their lives will be more than two or three years from the present. As teachers assess students, they need to be sensitive to their students' levels of development and make their assessments relevant to them. As teachers think about grading students and holding them accountable, they need to keep in mind that it may be more important to get the students to do the work rather than to give them a zero and tell them that they cannot make it up. Some teachers are concerned that they should not accept late work because they need to teach their students a lesson about meeting deadlines and being responsible. Teachers need to keep in mind two things. First, their students are still young and not developmentally sophisticated enough for the same standards as adults. Second, there are many examples in the real world that tell us just because you fail to meet a deadline, you still have to do what is expected. For example, just because you might be late paying a bill, you still have to pay it. As a matter or fact, you usually have to pay even more. Teachers should avoid giving zeroes, but they should also make sure students do the assigned work. Most often parents or administrators will help the teacher insist that students complete the work. For more discussion of this important aspect of differentiated assessment, see Wormeli (2006). If teachers cannot find a way to get students to do the work, they could at least use a point system that counteracts the devastating effects of putting a zero in the average.

Looking at Assessment Examples through the Lens of the Cognitive Process Dimension by Anderson and Colleagues

The work of Anderson, et al. (2001), also known as "New Bloom" informs the measurable objectives segment of the assessment explanation. When Anderson and colleagues revised Bloom's Taxonomy, they devised a method of categorizing cognitive processes that seems highly relevant to planning differentiated assessment. See their book for a full discussion of their ideas; however, here is a quick summary of their 6 main categories and 19 subcategories and how a teacher might address them through differentiated assessment. In Figure 1.11, I have summarized their definitions of cognitive processes and included how the teacher might differentiate the assessment of these processes.

Figure 1.11. Updated Bloom by Anderson, et al. (2001)

1. **Remember**—Retrieving information from the long-term memory		
1.1 Recognition	Defined as: Matching presented information with knowledge located in long-term memory. Also known as *identifying*.	Differentiating assessment: True/False, forced choice (multiple choice is the most popular), and matching are the three types. To differentiate these kinds of assessments the teacher might use games and tournaments to make them more engaging for all types of learners.
1.2 Recalling	Defined as: Getting relevant information from long-term memory. Also known as *retrieving*.	Differentiating assessment: To make this type of cognition most relevant to various learners, the teacher may embed the recall task in a larger high-interest problem.
2. **Understand**—Constructing meaning from instruction *Important:* If the teacher is to assess any higher-level cognitive function, the material presented must be new so that the student cannot rely on memory instead of higher-level thinking.		
2.1 Interpreting	Defined as: Changing from one type of representation to another. Also known as *clarifying, paraphrasing*.	Differentiating assessment: Assessment formats in which the teacher presents information in one form and students either construct or select the same information in a different form. Having students construct the information will elevate the assessment for advanced students. Struggling learners may feel more successful if the teacher allows them to select the answer.
2.2 Exemplifying	Defined as: Finding examples of a concept or principle. Also known as *illustrating*.	Differentiating assessment: This category provides an opportunity for the teacher to infuse artistic methods of constructing an answer to demonstrate cognitive mastery.
2.3 Classifying	Defined as: Deciding if something belongs to a category. Also known as: *categorizing, subsuming*.	Differentiating assessment: To assess learning students must either select a response or participate in a sorting task. Using a sorting task to place items in multiple categories can make this category a high-level learning experience for advanced students. Selecting a response makes it easier for struggling students.

2.4 Summarizing	Defined as: Determining a general theme or major points. Also known as *generalizing*.	Differentiating assessment: Teachers can make this category a high-level assessment experience for advanced students by asking them to construct information that is theme-based conceptualization rather than a summary of facts or events. Teachers can make it easier for struggling students by teaching them step by step methods of summarizing using graphic organizers and direct instruction.
2.5 Inferring	Defined as: Drawing logical conclusions from presented information. Also known as *predicting*.	Differentiating assessment: Common assessments for this cognitive category are completion tasks, analogy tasks, and oddity tasks. One way to make these assessments higher level for advanced students is to ask them to explain their underlying thinking for choosing their answer. One way to scaffold these tasks for struggling students is to provide lists of possible answers to complete the sentence or analogy.
2.6 Comparing	Defined as: Determining correspondence between ideas. Also known as *contrasting, matching*.	Differentiating assessment: Using cognitive-mapping strategies with some of the map filled in can provide scaffolding for struggling learners. Asking students to determine a full list of criteria on which to base comparing and contrasting can make this process higher level for advanced students.
2.7 Explaining	Defined as: Noting the cause and effect of something. Also known as constructing models.	Differentiating assessment: There are several possible assessment tasks for this cognitive category: reasoning, troubleshooting, redesigning, and predicting. All of these tasks can be designed to challenge the advanced learner because the problem through which they need to reason, or troubleshoot, redesign, or predict based on a change can be high level. The teacher may provide struggling students with scaffolding, such as helpful examples and partial completion of steps.

3. **Apply**—Using information or procedure in a situation		
3.1 Executing	Defined as: Using a procedure to perform a familiar task. Also known as *carrying out*.	Differentiating assessment: In this cognitive category teachers may differentiate the assessment based on the complexity and detail involved in addressing a specific task. Teachers might also provide graphic organizers to scaffold the task solution process for struggling learners.
3.2 Implementing	Defined as: Using a procedure to perform an unfamiliar task. Also known as *using*.	Differentiating assessment: The teacher may level these assessment tasks according to their difficulty. Teachers may also provide scaffolding organizers to help struggling students with procedures.
4. **Analyze**—Breaking something into parts to determine the purpose of the parts in relation to the overall purpose of the whole		
4.1 Differentiating	Defined as: Distinguishing between relevant and irrelevant parts of presented material. Also known as *discriminating*.	Differentiating assessment: Teachers may use a *constructed response* in which they give the students materials from which to choose to solve the task, and the students must decide which materials they need; or *selection task,* which asks students to determine which parts of the information provided about the task are relevant. The teacher can differentiate this assessment based on the "fuzziness" of the problems the students must solve. For advanced students the task may be complex, and for struggling students the task might be less fuzzy and require more guidance from the teacher in the way of organizers and other teacher input.
4.2 Organizing	Defined as: Deciding how elements fit or function within a structure or imposing a structure on material. Also known as *structuring*.	Differentiating assessment: To differentiate this cognitive category the teacher might use differing levels of material to ask students to outline. Or the teacher might make a selection task more challenging by asking students to select the best hierarchies from which to organize the leveled materials.

4.3 Attributing	Defined as: Determining what might be underlying presented material (e.g., author's purpose). Also known as *deconstructing*.	Differentiating assessment: Teachers may differentiate the assessment of this cognitive category based on the material from which they ask the students to construct or select a response. Also constructing a response from a prompt such as "Explain the author's purpose for writing this poem" can be more challenging than selecting that purpose from a list of purposes. It might also be easier to select from a different type of selection process in which the student decides if the author would agree or disagree with a specific statement the teacher makes about the material.
5. Evaluate—Making a judgment based on criteria		
5.1 Checking	Defined as: Determining the following: inconsistencies, effectiveness, consistency within a process or product. Also known as *testing*.	Differentiating assessment: The teacher may differentiate this cognitive assessment category by asking struggling students to check operations or products the teacher supplies. The teacher might also allow them to complete this kind of assignment in a small group with stronger students or with a stronger partner. The teacher might also give possible selection ideas. Teachers can make this process higher level by asking advanced students to check the accuracy and quality of products or processes they have created themselves.
5.2 Critiquing	Defined as: Determining the inconsistencies and appropriateness of a product or process based on external criteria. Also known as *judging*.	Differentiating assessment: To make this type of assessment easier, the teacher might provide the list of simple (positive and negative) criteria on which the students must judge a teacher-determined process or product. To make it harder the teacher might ask students to judge their own hypotheses or creations based on complex criteria they determine.

6. **Create**—Inserting new or reorganizing old elements to form a functional whole		
6.1 Generating	Defined as: Coming up with another idea based on criteria. Also known as *hypothesizing.*	Differentiating assessment: The teacher may differentiate these two subtypes of assessments for this cognitive category: *consequences tasks* (in which students list all the possible consequences of a specified event) and *uses tasks* (in which the student lists all the possible uses for an object). The teacher might differentiate this assessment by using events and objects that are highly relevant, well-known, and interesting to at-risk students. For example, the teacher might use a pop culture or sports event or object from which students must generate their lists. The teacher can make this assessment more challenging by making it more abstract and fuzzy for advanced learners.
6.2 Planning	Defined as: Determining a process for solving a problem. Also known as *designing.*	Differentiating assessment: To assess this cognitive category teachers might make it easier for struggling students by asking them to explain the plan for a solution that the teacher has already worked out, or teachers might provide an organizer to help the students describe a plan for a solution. The easiest assessment method could be that the students must select the correct solution plan for a given problem. To make this assessment more challenging, the teacher might ask students to develop a plan for a real world fuzzy problem they have decided to actually solve.
6.3 Producing	Defined as: Inventing something. Also known as *constructing.*	Differentiating assessment: The best way to assess this cognitive category is to ask students to design something based on specific criteria. Teachers can scaffold this category by providing graphic organizers that outline the steps and criteria clearly. Teachers can also break the task down into checkpoints that include making sure students are on the right track. To make this assessment more challenging teachers might make it a completely open-ended and fuzzy process in which the students are completely free to invent based on criteria they determine individually or as a class.

How to Use this Book

Chapter 1 provides an overview of differentiating assessment including the six parts involved in planning differentiated assessment. Chapter 2 provides an overview of types of assessment strategies. Chapters 3 through 5 provide specific differentiated assessment strategies in readiness and learning and thinking styles. And, Chapter 6 shows how the teacher might use several types of assessment in one unit of study.

The differentiation examples are a combination of ideas from many sources including my own *Handbook on Differentiating Instruction in Middle and High School* (Northey, 2005). The outline of formative assessments, however, uses the organizational structure from Silver, Strong, and Perini (2007) because although their book focuses on strategic and research-based *instruction* rather than assessment, the lessons they describe appear to be core and strategic methods of instruction that enhance the potential for differentiating assessment. (For other examples of how to use the strategies, you might see their book, *The Strategic Teacher: Selecting the Right Research-Based Strategy for Every Lesson.*)

Summary

This chapter provides an overview of crucial issues that stress the importance of including differentiated assessment as a major part of instruction. It shows the interaction among learning, assessment, and evaluation, defines differentiated assessment, explains how teachers might use a six part process to plan differentiated assessments, and provides an overview of the new version of Bloom's Taxonomy. It is important for teachers to remember that we have moved into the 21st Century and traditional thinking about how to plan instruction and how to assess student learning is changing. If teachers make differentiating assessment a priority, their students will have a better chance of gaining access to the culture of achievement that is necessary for surviving and thriving in our global society.

Note: Some of the strategies explained in this book are from a collection of assessment ideas I have gathered as a teacher. I have made every effort to determine their sources; however, if the originators of any of them feel they need to be cited, please contact me.

2

Types and Examples of Differentiated Assessments

Theorists and practitioners describe in several ways the types of assessments teachers can use to measure student achievement. This chapter provides an overview of these ways of describing them, and it provides examples of general assessment methods. As teachers begin to plan assessments, they need to think of themselves as assessors rather than activity designers. Figure 2.1 provides guidance.

Figure 2.1. Two Different Approaches to Assessment

Thinking Like an Assessor	*Thinking Like an Activity Designer*
What would be acceptable evidence of understanding?	What activities would be interesting and engaging as we learn about this topic?
What types of performance tasks will anchor the unit and focus the students' work?	What resources and materials do I have and need to teach this topic?
How can I tell who is really learning this versus who seems to be learning it?	What assignments will I give, homework and class work?
What criteria will I use to judge students' work?	How will I grade students and justify those grades to their parents?
What misunderstandings might students have and how can I check for them?	Did the activities work?

Adapted from Wiggins & McTighe (1998), p. 68.

Evaluation of Student Learning

The information in Figure 2.1 falls into the area of assessment, but what about evaluation? At what point do teachers decide what is acceptable evidence of learning, and what should they do with that evidence? Determining acceptable evidence that students have learned is a serious consideration, and teachers should take care to know when and why they are assessing what students know, what they can do, and what their attitudes are about their learning. Trussell-Cullen (1998) offers this excellent idea to help us decide some important questions about assessment. He proposes an "assessment audit" (Figure 2.2) that may help us develop a realistic perspective about the purpose(s) of assessments or evaluations of students' achievement in school.

Figure 2.2. Assessment Audit

Who is the test for?	What do they need the information for?	What kind of information do they need?
Teachers should have a clear idea of which stakeholders will be interested in the results of assessments. For most teachers stakeholders include students, parents, principals, district officials, and policy makers. The teacher is also included in this list.	This is an important question because different stakeholders may want assessments for varying reasons.	Once teachers have the answers to the first two questions, they can begin to determine the kinds of assessments to use and how they might organize and explain the results for the benefit of students.

Strategic Teaching: Assessments

Silver, Strong, & Perini (2007) have a model for differentiating instruction that includes five types of learning strategies to meet various learners' needs. These strategies include: mastery strategies, interpersonal strategies, understanding strategies, self-expression strategies, and four-style strategies. Figure 2.3 is a chart that focuses on the assessment aspect of the strategies they explain. In Chapters 3 through 5, teachers will learn specific examples of some of these strategies.

Figure 2.3. Model of Strategic Teaching—Silver, Strong, & Perini (2007)

Strategy	*Assessment*
Mastery Strategies	
New American lecture is a revision of the old lecture method that includes brain-based interactions that promote retention of concepts covered. (Ausubel, 1963, 1968)	The teacher stops at least every five minutes to ask questions that require a different style of thought. Teachers pose a problem that requires students to synthesize their learning from the lecture, assign a project, or use a traditional comprehension test.
Direct instruction is a four-phase process that results in independent learning. (updated Madeline Hunter by Robin Hunter)	The four phases are: modeling, direct practice, guided practice, and independent practice. This process encourages students to practice what they are learning without being afraid of grades. The teacher may assess students as they learn.
Graduated difficulty is a way to differentiate based on readiness. (Mosston, 1972)	The teacher designs tasks that are leveled: easy, medium, and hard. Students choose the level of difficulty and self-assess for mastery. Teachers may assess students' choices and movement toward mastery.
Teams-games-tournaments— Students compete with same-level students by answering questions to earn points for their home group. (DeVries, Edwards, & Slaven, 1978)	Teachers or students create question and answer cards that reflect the core ideas for reviewing a unit. They divide the students into heterogeneous home groups that include low, medium, and high students. Students prepare each other for the competition. Teachers assess the growth of individuals and groups.

Understanding Strategies	
Compare and contrast—Using various graphic organizers, show how various concepts and ideas are similar or different. (Marzano, Pickering, & Pollack, 2001)	Strategy includes four phases. Students: (1) Observe or read, (2) compare using a graphic organizer, (3) draw conclusions about comparisons, and (4) apply learning about comparisons. Assess at stages 2, 3, 4.
Reading for meaning—Using prereading, active reading, and postreading processes aid reading comprehension. (Herber, 1970)	Involves at least 10 types of reading strategies: vocabulary, determining main idea, inferring, forming claims or making a case, visualizing, making connections, exploring metaphor and symbol, attending to author's style, empathizing, and developing perspective. Assessment could be oral or written.
Concept attainment includes determining similarities and differences and testing hypotheses. (Bruner, 1973)	Teachers choose a concept for students to explore. They decide what examples fit into "yes," and which ones fit "no," to infer the critical attributes of the concept. Assessment includes products or tasks that show students' understanding of the concept.
Mystery—Students solve a problem or address a task by evaluating and using clues. Problem-based learning is a type of mystery learning. (Suchman, 1966)	Teachers determine a problem or task and clues that address a solution. Students make hypotheses that help solve the problem or complete the task. Assessment includes students' presentations of findings and solutions.

Self-Expression Strategies	
Inductive learning is a brainstorming and predicting process that includes grouping, labeling, and generalizing to construct central ideas. (Taba, 1971)	Teachers determine a possible generalization that they want students to discover through inductive reasoning. Assessment includes students completing a task demonstrating their understanding of the generalization.
Metaphorical expression— Students make meaning through a creative process of comparison. Other sources call this *synectics*. (Gordon, 1961)	Teachers introduce the central metaphor and then facilitate the students in developing a personal analogy, examining compressed conflicts, and extending their analogies. Assessment can be writing, developing a project, or other synthesis of the process.
Pattern maker (also known as *extrapolation*) is a way to help students see the way ideas and texts are structured or orga- nized so that they might use those structures to create or problem solve. (Gick & Holyoak, 1980)	Teachers introduce the analogue (information source of a pattern), help students see its pattern(s), and then help students apply that pattern to new material. Assessment would include determining how well students accurately identify the structure of the analogue and apply that understanding to solve a problem or create a product.
Mind's eye—Students visualize text to help them make predictions that they test with a text. It facilitates deep under- standing of a text. Alternative is visualing to problem solve. (Keene & Zimmerman, 1997)	Teachers tell students they will make movies in their minds as a text is read. Teachers then ask students to draw a picture, ask a question, make a prediction, or describe a feeling as an end product. Next teachers read 20 to 30 preselected words or phrases from the text slowly and with feeling. Assessment is the product (picture, ques- tion, etc.) and students' ability to compare that product to what they find in the text.

Interpersonal strategies	
Reciprocal learning—Students coach each other through the process of learning new information. Learning is doubled through this process. (Silver, Strong, & Perini, 2007)	Teachers create a reciprocal learning assignment and break students into pairs with one being A and the other, B. Teachers model the coaching process, and then troubleshoot while one student coaches the other one as he or she completes half of the assignment or a separate one, and then they switch roles. Assessment is the completion of the assignment and each student's ability to demonstrate successful coaching.
Decision making—Students get "inside" topics when the teacher asks them to make decisions about it. (Silver, Strong, & Perini, 2007)	Teachers set up a situation that requires students to make decisions and then help them identify sources of information, develop criteria, and decide how to communicate their decisions. Assessment is the quality of that communication.
Jigsaw is a cooperative learning strategy in which students read and report to their home group on a part of a reading task. (Aronson, Blaney, Stephen, Sikes, & Snapp, 1978)	Teachers determine an assignment (usually reading), divide students into cooperative home groups, and have groups number off. All the ones (twos, etc.) read the same part of the assignment and then talk about how to communicate what they learned to their home group. Assessment of learning from jigsaw can be a test on the materials.
Community circle helps students build a sense of community as they learn about themselves through sharing their thoughts, feelings, and values. (Silver, Strong, & Perini, 2007)	Assessment occurs when teachers help students reflect on what came out in the discussion. Students self-assess and give helpful feedback (nonjudgmental) to each other.

Four-Style Strategies	
Window notes expand the process of note taking to include not only the facts about a topic, but also the students' feelings, questions, and ideas about that topic. (Silver, Strong, & Perini, 2007)	Teachers ask students to divide a sheet of paper into four sections and label them as follows: facts, feelings, questions, ideas. When students read something, they make notes including information for each of the sections. Assessment is the teacher's evaluation of the notes.
Circle of Knowledge, also known as Socratic Seminar if it is text-based, is a strategy that promotes academic discussion. (Silver, Strong, & Perini, 2007)	Teachers ask students to discuss a topic in a scholarly manner. Assessment can be a method of crediting students for making high-quality remarks about the topic, and for Socratic Seminar, referencing the text, which is a great method for oral language practice including use of standard English.
Do you hear what I hear? Students listen to teacher read a selection of information and then respond to what they heard (Strong, Silver, Perini, & Tuculescu, 2002).	Teachers choose a selection of information to read to the class. Students just listen to the first reading, and then take notes on the second reading. Assessment is students showing what they know from what they heard in a variety of products or performances.
Task rotation—Students choose from a variety of mastery, understanding, self-expression, or interpersonal tasks. (Silver, Strong, & Perini, 2007)	Teachers determine a variety of tasks from which students can choose to show what they have learned. Assessment is differentiated naturally because students can choose how they want to show what they know.

Adapted from *The Strategic Teacher: Selecting the Right Research-Based Strategy for Every Lesson,* by H. Silver, W. Strong, & M. Perini, 2007, Alexandria, VA: Association for Supervision and Curriculum Development.

Types of Assessments

Practitioners and theorists often refer to three types of assessment: preassessment, formative assessment, and summative assessment. I have added informal and affective assessment. Figure 2.4 is an overview of how they are evaluated, when they are used, and their major purposes.

Figure 2.4. Five Types of Assessments

Type	Grading/ Evaluating	When Used	Purpose
Preassessment	A check mark for participation: + = high quality; − = low quality	Before learning	1. Lets teachers know what their students already understand, know, and can do related to the topic or concept. 2. Helps teachers decide what they need to include in their unit. 3. Piques students' interest in the unit.
Informal assessment	A check mark for participation: + = high quality; − = low quality	During learning	1. Allows teachers to take whole class and individual assessments that are quick and easy to note. 2. These assessments can evaluate cognitive or affective growth.
Formative assessment	Can be a check mark with pluses and minuses or A, B, and N (for "needs work" or "not yet")	During learning	1. Helps teachers adjust their instruction so that students have a better chance of learning. 2. Allows teachers to constantly check to see what their students understand, know, and can do. 3. Provides an opportunity for teachers to give students clear and comprehensive feedback on their learning to date.

Type	Grading/ Evaluating	When Used	Purpose
Summative assessment	Grades such as A,B,C, D. & F or "Not Yet" or "Needs work"	After learning	Allows teachers and students to know how successful they were when the unit is completed. May help teachers adjust instruction for the future and may provide information that suggests remediation for students.
Affective assessment	Not graded Sutdents write reflections in "Learning Logs" that the teacher reads and checks off	Before, during, and after learning	*Answers these questions:* How interesting is this topic to each student? What do students believe and feel about what they have learned? How does this learning affect students as learners? Provides teachers constant access to how students are reacting emotionally to the unit. Assess often.

Keeping these ideas in mind, the following sections are some examples of assessments that would fit any situation in any content.

Preassessments: Literacy Readiness

One of the most important things a middle or high school teacher needs to know about his or her students is how literate each student is in the subject area the teacher is teaching them. Not only do teachers need to know how well students can read and understand the major materials (usually a textbook) the teacher uses to teach the class, they also need to know how well students have incorporated the core structures and protocols of that subject area. [See Northey (2005) for several ways to assess students' reading level.] Teachers may use standardized test results to help them determine reading levels, or if they have reasons to believe the student may not be able to read at grade level, they may refer the student for a thorough reading assessment. If the school uses "Accelerated Reader," teachers can use the "Star Test" to determine students' lexile levels. The teacher may want to take some time with individual students to get a good idea for how well that student reads. Sometimes the teacher is surprised that students read their text so poorly. If the teacher knows a student has difficulty reading a text independently, he or she must find alternative materials or provide significant scaffolding to help the student access the text.

Reading Aloud

It is critical that teachers know how well students can read the materials from which they teach. Teachers often use round-robin reading as a classroom management tool or as a way to assure that everyone in the class is reading and understanding the text. Brain-based research and other reading research tell us that round-robin reading is an ineffective reading method. The most compelling reason, among many others, is that according to brain-based research, when students are reading aloud, the area in the brain that is comprehending the text (making meaning) is in competition with the parts of the brain that are controlling speaking and other physiological aspects that occur when a student reads aloud. In other words, it is difficult for students to read aloud and comprehend what they are reading. Also, depending on the reading ability of the student reading aloud, especially his or her fluency, the students who are listening may not be able to comprehend the text. There are many other wonderful methods of oral reading and shared reading that teachers might use. Here are two excellent titles: *Good-bye Round Robin: 25 Effective Oral Reading Strategies* by Michael Opitz and Timothy Rasinski (1998) and *Strategies for Integrating Reading and Writing* by Karen Wood (2001).

Preassessments: Learning Styles

When teachers plan to differentiate assessment, they need to have a full range of learning styles inventories from which to choose. See my books, *Handbook on Differentiating Instruction in Middle and High School* (Northey, 2005) and *The Democratic Differentiated Classroom* (Waterman, 2007) for several learning styles inventories. See Chapter 1 for an overview of learning and thinking styles.

Preassessments: Interests

Assessing interest in a topic can be a matter of asking students in a short survey about their interest in a specific part of a unit of study and in the unit of study as a whole. The survey could be as simple as asking the following:

- ◆ Rate your interest in this topic from 1 (no interest) to 10 (very interested).
- ◆ If you are not very interested in this topic, what would make you more interested in it? Please be specific.

Knowing if students have a fundamental interest or disinterest in the topic can help teachers adjust assessments so that motivation is optimal.

Preassessments: Content

Anticipation Guide (Herber, 1978)

Many textbooks have interesting true/false guides in their ancillary resources, but teachers can also construct these for any unit or topic. The teacher writes a few (no more than 10) statements that could be true or false about the unit or topic. Students make their best guess to determine if the statements are true or false. After students have made their best guesses, they read the source of information and correct their misconceptions. This guide can create curiosity and motivation to read for understanding.

Five Question Preassessment Quiz

This is a great way to start a unit and to engage students in a unit of study. The teacher chooses five questions that might pique students' interest in a topic and might give the teacher a good idea of what they already know about it. The discussion that follows this preassessment quiz, if handled correctly, can get any unit off to an exciting start.

KWL (Adaptation) (Ogle, 1986)

Teachers who use this strategy should make a chart with a big K for what we already know, W for what we want to learn, and L for how we want to learn. This is a perfect strategy for teachers to learn the extent of some of the students' background knowledge of a topic. The teacher needs to keep in mind, however, that just because one or more students place an idea in the K box does not mean that all students have that K. The W is an excellent place to help students learn to develop essential questions (EQs) for the unit. The L helps the teachers know how certain members of the class want to learn about the topic. This information is also helpful for designing formative assessments.

The teacher might also adapt the KWL to help gather important information about what individual students know and can do regarding the topic of a unit of study. To use this method most effectively the teacher should know what skills are required to learn about the topic, and what skills students might learn or develop as they explore the unit. The teacher should also have a clear idea of the knowledge students will gain by exploring this unit.

It is also important that students prove they can do the things they say they can do, and that they know the things they say they know. In addition to the survey, therefore, the teacher should also include a sample problem attached to the pretest and a typical problem attached to the posttest. These sample problems will verify that students can in fact do what they say they can do and that they know what they say they know.

By preassessing and postassessing, the teacher and student will have a better idea about the learning that took place. The students might actually count the number of skills and knowledge they listed before and after studying the unit, thus quantifying the amount of learning. They could also use a rating scale to quantify attitudes, interests, and feelings.

Figure 2.5. Know and Do Pre- and Post-Assessment

Adaptation of the KWL

Name: _____ Date:_____

Topic of Unit: _____

1. I know how to:

    (Complete this stem by listing skills related to learning about this unit of study.)

2. How many ideas did you list?_____

3. I know that:

    (Complete this stem by listing information and ideas you know about this unit of study.)

4. How many ideas did you list?_____

5. Write one or two sentences explaining your general knowledge about and interest in this unit of study.

6. Rate your general knowledge and interest in this unit of study (1 being lowest and 10 being highest): _____

7. Write one or two sentences explaining how you feel about exploring this unit of study.

8. Rate your feelings about exploring this unit of study (1 being lowest and 10 being highest):
    Total score:_

9. Complete the assignment attached to this form.

Keeping Track of Learning

Students might track their learning for the year using the format in Figure 2.6.

Figure 2.6. Track My Learning

Tracking My Learning in_____ for School Year_____

Write the title of each unit of study in the spaces below. Record the dates of study in the appropriate boxes. Record your total score (from your preassessment and post-assessment from your Know and Do Pre- and Post-Assessment forms) in the appropriate boxes.

Title of Unit of Study	Dates of Study	Prescore	Post-Score

Looking at this quantitative measure of your learning over the year, what conclusions can you draw?

3-2-1

The teacher might preassess what students already know, what they want to learn, and any other information by using a 3-2-1 activity. The teacher may also use this strategy as a summative assessment. To use it as a preassessment, the teacher may give students an index card or ask them to write the information on their own paper and then ask them to list the following:

- ◆ 3 things you want to learn about this topic
- ◆ 2 questions you have about it
- ◆ 1 way you want to learn about it (i.e., writing, researching, group activities, etc.)

Quick Write (Rief, 1998)

To preassess what students already know about a topic, the teacher might ask them to write (without stopping) for 5 to 10 minutes about the topic. The teacher might also use this with a partner. For instance the teacher asks the students to write everything they know about at topic and then exchange papers with a partner. Following this exercise, the teacher may then ask partners to share at least one important idea they already know about the topic.

Interview

The teacher might give students an interview template and ask them to find out what at least three students in the class already know about the topic. They might then turn the template in so that the teacher can get a better idea about what students already know. Students can also take turns sharing what they found out in their interviews.

Informal Assessments

Informal assessments are defined here as quick checks for understanding that the teacher can use without a great deal of preparation or development of an instrument. The two major types of informal assessments are (1) pop or announced, short written quizzes and (2) oral or other impromptu quickly written checks for understanding at the beginning, middle, or end of classroom instruction. Informal assessments are great ways to determine if all students are learning *while* the teacher is instructing them. If the teacher does not have a good idea of how students are learning on a daily basis, he or she may inadvertently move forward and leave one, several, or the majority of the class behind.

Pop or Announced Short Written Quizzes

Five-Question Quiz to Start or End the Class

If the teacher uses a quick written quiz as an informal assessment to check if students have understood and retained the information addressed in the lesson, there are a few ideas to consider as follows:

♦ Use a five-question quiz based on the essential ideas of the previous or current day's lesson. These questions should capture the critical concepts included in the lesson. They should be questions that teachers can quickly determine and with which they may be flexible depending on what they in fact were able to cover in the lesson.

♦ The teacher could grade the quiz as follows: A+ for all correct, A– for one missed, B for two missed, C for three missed, D for four missed, and F for all missed.

- The teacher may count these as quiz grades (not weighted) or may use them to learn if students have gaps in their understanding of concepts.

- The teacher should collect the quizzes in a predetermined amount of time, not allowing students to use more time than allotted. They will get use to the idea that the teacher is timing the quiz, and they know the information or they don't. Giving this kind of informal assessment is a great way to settle and quiet a class in the beginning and at the end of the class.

- The five-question quiz fits well into any lesson plan because teachers may use it for review at the beginning or end of any class.

Oral or Other Impromptu Checks for Understanding

According to Fisher and Frey (2007), oral assessment is a wonderful way to check for understanding; however, there are several issues to consider when using this kind of informal assessment: "poverty, language, and perceived skill level; gender differences; and the initiate-respond-evaluate (IRE) model of questioning" (p. 21). Fisher and Frey (2007) cite several studies that show the following: Teachers do most of the talking in all classes, but they do even more talking in classes of at-risk students.

- Teachers call on girls less and less as they get older. They call on boys more often and ask them higher-level questions.

- The IRE model that has been in teachers' practices for years is ineffective because it does not focus on critical thinking for *all* students. It goes like this: I—teacher asks a question, R—students try to guess the answer the teacher is looking for, and E—the teacher makes an evaluative statement, such as, "great answer" or "no, that is not correct."

The following sections offer strategies and solutions to these problems identified by Fisher and Frey (2007, pp. 21–35).

Noticing Nonverbal Cues

Remembering that much of our communication is nonverbal, teachers can be alert to the looks on students' faces and other nonverbal cues to help them informally assess learning. Some students may be too shy to call attention to their misunderstanding; however, if the teacher notices a puzzled look on a student's face, he or she might provide a less embarrassing way for the student to get clarification.

Whip Around

Fisher and Frey (2007) suggest that "Whip Around" is a great informal way to find out if a group of students is following the instruction and what misconceptions or gaps might exist in their learning. Here is how it goes:

1. At the end of instruction, the teacher asks students a question that might have at least three parts to the answer, or the teacher asks students to list at least three things they learned about the lesson.

2. The teacher asks students to write their three things on a scrap piece of paper.

3. The teacher then tells students to stand up when they have finished writing their three things. He or she tells them that when they have heard all the items on their scrap of paper mentioned, they should sit down.

4. Next, the teacher calls on one student at a time to read one of the items on their scrap of paper.

5. The teacher tells students that if they hear an item they have listed, they should cross it off their list, but that they should remain standing until at least one student has mentioned the item.

6. The teacher continues to call on students until all are seated.

By following this process, the teacher can note any significant ideas that students left out.

Whole-Class Hand Signals

A way to check to see if all students understand, know, or can do some aspect of a topic or concept is through hand signals.

Method One

Students answer a question or work a problem. The teacher instructs students to do the following:

1. Put a fist in front of your chest.

2. Indicate agreement with the answer or solution by putting a thumb up, indicate disagreement with the answer or solution by putting a thumb down, and indicate ambivalence with the answer or solution by making the hand wiggle back and forth.

Method Two

The teacher asks a question with A, B, C, or D as answers

1. Put a fist in front of the chest.

2. Indicate the correct letter using American Sign Language to designate A, B, C, or D.

Method Three: Seven Hands Raised

After a teacher asks a question, she says she will not get an answer until seven people have raised their hands. She then calls on one of them to answer (Smith, 2004).

Waiting until seven hands are raised does two things: (1) forces wait time and (2) assures that more students are taking responsibility for oral assessment.

Method Four

The teacher asks students to close their eyes and then to rate their understanding of the lesson as follows: 3 = excellent understanding, 2 = moderate understanding, and 1 = poor understanding. She asks students to hold up their hands when the teacher calls the number of their rating. For instance, when the teacher calls out 3, all students who have an excellent grasp on the lesson will raise their hands (Allen, 2007).

An adaptation of this method is that students should put a 1, 2, or 3 in front of their bodies to show how well they have understood the lesson.

Whole Class Movement

Four Corners

The teacher asks a question and gives four possible answers. Each answer is assigned a corner of the room. Students go to the corner with which they agree.

White-Board Assessments

Students use a marker to work a problem or answer a question on a small white board.

Method One

Students work individually or with a partner.
1. The teacher asks a question or states a problem.
2. Students record their answers on the white board with a marker.
3. When the teacher says, "hold up your answer," each student holds up the white board with his or her answer on it.

Method Two

Students work individually or with a partner.
1. The teacher assigns each person or partners a sentence to write, problem to work, or other.
2. Students record their work on a white board.
3. Students share their work as a presentation before the class.
4. Class members put thumbs up or thumbs down to assess agreement or disagreement with students' solutions.

Method Three

The teacher might use a new technology that provides handheld small white boards of slates on which students might record answers that can be uploaded onto a large white board at the front of the class.

Demand Response

Names in Basket

Teachers get a small basket for each of their classes and put each student's name in it. The teacher asks a question and pulls a name out of the basket to decide on whom to call. A standard follow-up question, "Why is that your answer?" takes the process automatically to a higher level of thinking.

The following are ways to differentiate demand response for struggling students:

- Allow them to "phone a friend"

- Ask an opinion question

- Preview the question and its answer in a "secret" conversation

- Ask a struggling student to share his or her answer when you have walked around and noticed that he or she has written a good answer

- Call on a student when you know he or she has a good answer even if you have not actually pulled his or her name. No one knows whose name is really being pulled.

- Acccept "I don't know the answer *yet*," and then prompt the student to figure it out.

Formative Assessments

Using Formative Assessments to Prepare Students for Standardized Tests

Many teachers make faulty assumptions about the best way to prepare students to take standardized tests during which students must read a selection and answer multiple-choice questions. They believe the best way to prepare students to take these tests is to use an outside source of reading selections (many varied reading selections are provided online or published in test-preparation books) that help them simulate the testing process. They ask students to read selections, answer the questions, and then go over the answers as a class. An alternative to this method includes the following two ideas:

1. Teachers can learn to write the kinds of questions that may be used on standardized tests. They should go online to obtain a list of question stems on

which their district or state bases its curriculum. They can then use their own content as selections for multiple-choice testing assessments. Teachers should make sure that deep learning is the goal and that using multiple-choice questions aligned with standardized tests are for building skill with these kinds of questions. Teachers might also give students stems from which to compose their own questions that align with standardized tests.

2. Teachers could use outside sources for reading selections; however, instead of asking students to read, and then immediately answer standardized questions, the teacher could use an instructional strategy or formative assessment to help students better understand the selection. Here is a general list of possible formative assessment activities:

   • Make a diagram of the plot or organizational style of the selection.

   • Make a cause and effect graphic organizer.

   • Draw pictures of various aspects of the selection that show comprehension.

   • Use Venn diagrams or other compare and contrast graphic organizers to make sure students understand the selection.

   • Use thinking maps, charts, or organizers to show reading comprehension.

   • Use outlining.

   • Use a "fact trap" to determine main idea and supporting details (Figure 2.7). From Patricia Gregory, "EOG Reading," Workshop, February 15, 2008.

Figure 2.7. Fact Trap

Supporting Details	Main Idea	Supporting Details

To make test preparation more like a learning process than *"skill and drill," teachers should use any assessment strategy that helps students comprehend the selection before moving to answering the standardized questions.* From Patricia Gregory, "EOG Reading," Workshop, February 15, 2008.

Cooperative Learning Formative Assessments

Cooperative learning activities can help teachers determine if individual students are learning; however, they must take special care to design assessments that provide individual data. Although cooperative learning activities should be interdependent, it is dangerous to give grades to individuals based on the work of the group. Teachers can, however, use various techniques to capitalize on group solidarity to inspire all members of the group to achieve. Here are helpful guidelines from Sagor and Cox (2004) on developing cooperative learning activities.

Step 1: The teacher decides what objective(s) to address and describes the product that will address that objective.

Step 2: The teacher decides why he or she wants to use cooperative learning.

Step 3: The teacher determines the roles that each person will have in each cooperative group.

Step 4: The teacher designs a method for individual accountability.

Figure 2.8 shows a few specific ideas about how to differentiate assessments from cooperative learning activities.

Figure 2.8. Differentiate Assessments from Cooperative Learning Activities

Structure	How to Do It	Differentiated Assessment Strategies
Numbered Heads Together (Kagen, 1997)	Students form small groups of four or five. The teacher asks questions, and the students consult with each other to decide on the answer. One student provides the answer.	1. The teacher makes the groups homogeneous based on similar academic achievement. 2. Specially differentiated questions are asked of each group. 3. Each student receives a participation check. 4. Quality designations are awarded (+ for exceptional and − for needs work)
Think-Pair-Share (Kagen, 1997)	The teacher poses a question or situation. Students are asked to think about it for a short time. Next, students find a partner to share what they have thought. Finally, the teacher asks for answers.	1. This is a great way to differentiate assessment and use the findings of brain-based research, which states that students learn best when they are not in a stressful situation. By allowing struggling students to discuss their thinking with another student, the teacher is greatly reducing the stress they might feel if they had to find the answers alone. 2. This is also a great way to capitalize on the idea that students learn from each other.
Pairs Check (Kagen, 1997)	Students form groups of four. Within that group, two students work as partners to solve problems. One works the problem while the other coaches. After every two problems, the pairs check to see if they have the same answers. Students may reverse roles or stay the same.	As with Think-Pair-Share this is a good stress reducer and a chance for students to learn from each other. It works nicely as a formative assessment because the teacher can tell if students understand how to solve the problems. Teachers might also use this strategy for answering questions on an assignment sheet.

Oral Formative Assessments

"Accountable Talk"

Teachers might improve oral assessments if they use a strategy cited in Fisher and Frey (2007) called "Accountable Talk," which was developed by Lauren Resnick (2000). It includes a list of agreements teachers and students make concerning student to student conversations. "Accountable Talk" includes the following three requirements that students learn, practice, and agree to maintain:

1. Staying on topic
2. Using information that is accurate and appropriate
3. Listening carefully and thinking about what others say

Accountable talk also requires students to follow these strategies that they learn, practice, and maintain for each non-teacher-led discussion:

1. Press the speaker to clarify and explain. "Could you describe what you mean?"
2. Require the speaker to justify proposals or challenges to others' proposals by referencing the source. "Where did you find that information?"
3. Challenge ideas that seem wrong "I don't agree because…"
4. Require the speaker to provide evidence for claims. "Can you give me an example?"
5. Use each other's statements. "Susan suggested… and I agree with her."

Values Lineup

Values lineup developed by Kagen and cited in Fisher and Frey (2007) is an excellent method for orally assessing how students feel about an academic topic. It also helps them practice expressing themselves orally. It goes like this:

1. The teacher prepares a statement or statements that represent the essential concepts of an academic topic.
2. Students evaluate the statement and position themselves in a line according to that evaluation (levels of agreement or disagreement).
3. The teacher then asks the students to fold the line in half so that the students at either ends of the continuum will talk to one another.

Retellings

Another great way to find out orally if students understand what they are reading is to use the process of retelling. To use this strategy, the teacher needs to teach students by doing the following:

1. Explain that retelling is the process of recreating a text in your own words.

2. Help students see that retelling something they have read in school is similar to telling a friend about a movie they have seen.

3. Model for students how to retell a piece of text.

4. Discuss with students the differences and similarities between the retelling and the actual text.

5. Select another text and ask students to practice retelling.

6. Once again compare the differences and similarities between the original text and the retelling.

According to Fisher and Frey (2007) there are many types of retelling as follows: oral to oral, oral to written, oral to video, reading to oral, reading to written, reading to video, viewing to oral, viewing to writing, viewing to video. Fisher and Frey also include a rubric for retellings in their book (2007, p. 29).

Assessment Tools

This section includes an overview of types of tools for evaluating student work, such as the following: rubrics, constructing multiple-choice tests, participation grid, portfolios.

Rubrics

Using and Designing Effective Rubrics

Teachers may easily go online to find a website that will help them design a rubric for any assessment they may be planning. Rubrics are excellent tools to evaluate a differentiated assessment of students' learning. There are two basic kinds of rubrics, analytical and holistic. Analytical rubrics break the description of the levels of performance into discrete parts whereas holistic rubrics list the parts as one whole statement or paragraph. One might use an analytical rubric for formative evaluation and a holistic rubric for summative evaluation. The best kind of rubric from my perspective is a "consensus rubric" (Waterman, 2006). This kind of rubric allows teachers to determine with the class what constitutes quality work. Here are the steps to working with students to design a consensus rubric:

Step 1: The teacher arranges the room in a circle if possible. Rows may work, but students will have a harder time talking to one another.

Step 2: The teacher hands each student a copy of the blank rubric chart (Figure 2.9) and tells them that the class will be working together to plan a consensus rubric.

Step 3: The teacher asks students to work alone or with a partner to determine categories for evaluating a certain assessment.

Step 4: The teacher asks students to share their ideas about categories with the whole class.

Step 5: The teacher should use voting to decide the top four categories. Some typical categories may be as follows: originality, content, organization, or technical quality.

Step 6: After the teacher has decided those categories, he or she should ask students this question: "What does a 4 look like?" He or she might start with the highest quality but could start anywhere. The class continues filling in the rubric until it is complete.

Note: The first time the class does this, the teacher may need to directly instruct and model for students what constitutes the most appropriate evaluative words and phrases. One way to do this is to analyze the words and phrases professional rubric-makers use.

Figure 2.9. How to Create a Consensus Rubric

Materials needed: (1) a blank rubric chart like this:

Category	Level 1	Level 2	Level 3	Level 4

One of the challenges with using rubrics is converting their scores to grades. Here is how to do it. For an analytical rubric, the teacher should give each category a point value. For instance in any rubric, each category could be worth 25 points each, or teachers could weight the points in some way, such as 20 points for writing, 20 points for organization, 50 points for accuracy, and 10 points for graphics. They should deduct points for each category based on the student's attainment of the rubric standards.

For example, for a "brochure project," Jane's brochure has the following features:

- For "writing/organization," each section has an exceptionally clear and thoughtful beginning, middle, and end. Score 25 points.

- For "attractiveness/organization," the brochure has attractive formatting, but it is not exceptional. There is one place that it is somewhat sloppy. Deduct 5 points. Score 20.

- For "content/accuracy," the student has made one error in accuracy. Deduct 1 point. Score 24.

- For "graphics/pictures," there are too many graphics and not enough text; however, the graphics do go with the text and there is one original graphic. Deduct 11 points. Score 14.

Scores are as follows:

Writing/organization	25
Attractiveness/organization	20
Content/accuracy	24
Graphics/pictures	14
Total score	83 = C or C+

For the holistic rubric the teacher could use the following scoring process:

4 = no loss of points = A+
3 = loss of 1–11 points = 89–99 = A, A–, or B+
2 = loss of 12–23 points = 88–77 = B, C+, or C
1 = loss of 24 or more points = 76–0 = D+, D, D–, or F

Or the teacher can say that Level 4 = A (well above average); Level 3 = B (above average); Level 2 = C (average); Level 1 = D (below average); and not doing the work at all is F or Not Yet.

Some systems consider 2 to be failing (below average) and 1 to be well below average. Also as mentioned previously, it is a good policy to avoid zeroes.

Designing rubrics has become quite easy with all the online sources available. The teacher might also encourage students to explore these rubric-making sites. Figure 2.10 is an annotated list of some of the best ones teachers may use.

Figure 2.10. Rubric-Making Websites

Website and Address	Description
RubiStar http://Rubistar.4teachers.org	A free tool to help teachers create excellent rubrics. Easy to use and comprehensive.
Teachnology: *The Web Portal for Educators* http://www.teach-nology.com/	Has free rubric-maker capacity for a wide variety of topics from behavior modification to evaluating oral projects.
Kathy Schrock's Guide for Educators http://schooldiscovery.com/schrockguide/assess.html.	Has excellent subject-specific and general rubrics and web-based rubrics that include assessing WebQuests, school web pages, classroom web pages, and student web pages.
Midlink Magazine Teacher Tools http://www.ncsu.edu/midlink/ho.html	Has a wide variety of multimedia rubrics, software evaluation rubrics, and many more.

Summative Assessment Tools—Tests

Most textbooks provide summative assessments for teachers to use; however, *it might be best for teachers to create their own unit tests based on their standard course of study and based on students' needs.* To construct a "fair" summative assessment for students, teachers might evaluate their assessment based on the following checklist (Figure 2.11). The idea of a checklist comes from Linn and Miller as cited in Fisher and Frey (2007). I have adapted their adaptation of Linn and Miller. See Fisher and Frey (2007) for a more thorough discussion of these kinds of assessments. Figures 2.11 through 2.16 are a series of possible checklists teachers might use to evaluate their assessments.

Figure 2.11. General Criteria

Check	Criteria
_____	I have picked a test that matches the way I taught this topic.
_____	I am assessing the essential knowledge and skills for this topic.
_____	My test does not require my students to read at a level that might prevent their showing me what they actually know and understand.
_____	There are no typos or mistakes in my test that would confuse students.
_____	My test does a good job of being culturally relevant and unbiased for my students.
_____	I have prepared my students for this test so that they should be adequately challenged, but not overwhelmed by it.
_____	The directions for taking the test are clear and easy to understand.

True/False Tests

To make these kinds of assessments fair, teachers should make sure they can check off these criteria:

Figure 2.12. True -False Tests

Check	Criteria
_____	The statements are only true or false, not partially true in some cases and false in others.
_____	The statements are appropriately challenging.
_____	The statements do not address opinions.
_____	The statements are similar in length.
_____	The statements include no double negatives.
_____	Each statement includes only one fact.

True/false questions are problematic because of guessing, which most students are accustomed to doing. One way to solve that problem is to require students to correct statements they believe are false.

Short Answer

To make these kinds of assessments fair for students, teachers should make sure they can check off these criteria:

Figure 2.13. Short Answer Questions

Check   **Criteria**

_____   The answers include a symbol, word, or phrase.

_____   The question does not give clues to the answer (such as an, a).

_____   The questions are in student-friendly language for at-risk students.

_____   The test leaves space for showing work.

Multiple Choice

To make these kinds of assessments fair for students, teachers should make sure they can check off these criteria:

Figure 2.14. Multiple Choice Tests

Check   **Criteria**

_____   The item stems are aligned with the objectives of the unit and with district or state curriculum standards.

_____   The item stems reflect a continuum of thinking skills.

_____   The stems are written in positive terms.

_____   The distracters are similar in length and style to the true answers.

_____   The items do not give clues to the correct answer.

_____   The stems are clear, specific, and unambiguous.

Matching

To make these kinds of assessments fair, teachers should make sure they can check off these criteria:

Figure 2.15. Matching

Check   **Criteria**

_____ The test does not include more than approximately 20 items.

_____ The test is all on one page.

_____ There is one match for each statement.

_____ I have taken the test myself to make sure everything matches.

This is a low-level testing process because the content must be based on facts to be successful.

Extended Writing Response

To make these kinds of assessments fair, teachers should make sure they can check off these criteria:

Figure 2.16. Extended Writing Response

Check   **Criteria**

_____ Students understand how I will evaluate the writing.

_____ Students know how much time they have to write their response.

_____ The writing prompt addresses higher-level thinking processes.

_____ The writing allows at-risk students to be successful even if their writing skills are weak.

_____ I have given students writing choices. (This is not mandatory, but it is a good idea.)

_____ I have written the response myself so I have some idea what students will write or should write.

Constructing Multiple-Choice Tests

Standardized tests are a current reality, and they have usually functioned as the primary gateway into colleges and universities; therefore, teachers must not ignore the importance of teaching their students the strategy of identifying best answers in multiple-choice tests (i.e., convergent reasoning). Teachers often have access to multiple-choice tests formats provided for them by their districts or provided in test-preparation workbooks; however, teachers can greatly increase their capability of providing multiple-choice question answering practice for her students by doing two things.

- Learning how to write high-level multiple-choice questions based on text-books and other print and nonprint resources
- Teaching students to write high-level multiple-choice questions themselves

Teachers Writing Their Own Tests

What follows are some steps that might help teachers write their own multiple-choice questions.

Step 1: Teachers should analyze the types of multiple-choice question stems standardized tests require their students to answer. They should then make a list of these stems if their school system does not provide them.

Step 2: As teachers read and go over the materials they have for their content area, they should use those stems to construct questions that address the most important aspects of their materials.

Step 3: Teachers should choose answers that for the most part *could* be true, but only one answer is *best.* These "could be true" answers are called distracters. The best kinds of distracters fall into one of these categories: misconception, oversimplification, or overgeneralization. Teachers should learn to write these distracters if they want to construct strong multiple-choice tests for their students. It is also a good idea to teach students how to write questions with appropriate distracters. This step can be tricky because questions need to be fair. Teachers should avoid questions that are based on opinion or that might reflect a bias. They should focus on questions that reflect the *best* interpretation or analysis. They should make sure they do not include more than one *correct* answer.

Step 4: Teachers should find a quick way to score these multiple-choice tests. The "bubble sheet" (see below) is a quick and easy way for students to respond to multiple-choice tests. If the school does not have bubble sheets or a scoring machine, here is how to make bubble sheets and how to score students' multiple-choice responses with one of them:

Making and Hand-Scoring a Multiple-Choice Test Bubble Sheet

Step 1: The teacher makes the test.

Step 2: Print enough copies of a "bubble sheet" for all class members and one for the key (use *Catpin.com* or other websites that construct bubble sheets).

Step 3: Teachers should take the test themselves (this will help discover any mistakes) to make the key.

Step 4: Laminate the key.

Step 5: Use a hole-puncher with a long neck or make slits down each row.

Step 6: Use a hole-puncher to punch out the correct answers on the key.

Step 7: Use a colored marker to mark students' incorrect answers on their test through the holes in the key. The teacher can quickly see how many questions students missed to determine their score.

Whole Class Oral Participation Assessments

When teachers use a whole-class oral assessment, such as a discussion group, they may want to track students' participation using the following grid (Figure 2.17). Some teachers announce student scores at the end of the discussion. Being able to announce high grades can be motivational for students but announcing low grades can have the opposite effect. Teachers may want to consider the culture of the class to decide if they want to do this.

Figure 2.17. Class Participation Grid

Student															Grade

Instructions: List all the students in the class. Put a plus sign or check mark for every positive comment a student makes in a class discussion and put a minus sign for every negative response a student makes during class discussion. Decide how many pluses or check marks constitute an A, B, C, D, or F. Deduct minuses from the total pluses or check marks.

Summary

This chapter provided several generic methods for differentiating assessment including ideas for pre-assessing, informally assessing, assessing affect, and formative and summative assessments. In the chapters that follow, teachers will see specific examples of these strategies.

3

Highly Structured English and Social Studies Assessments

This chapter shows teachers specific examples of differentiated assessment strategies that are leveled for students who have special readiness needs. After providing an overview of these students' special needs, it provides examples of preassessments, formative assessments, and summative assessments. For the formative assessments, it provides information about the Differentiating Assessment Six-Part Template. What follows is a thorough explanation of Part 1 for students who might need a highly structured assessment experience.

Students' Needs

Who Are the Students Who Need a Great Deal of Structure?

Students for whom we need to provide a great deal of structure in our assessments are called "at-risk," "struggling," or "priority" students. In this book, we will call them "at-risk" students because that term seems to be most descriptive. At-risk students include those who are at risk of failing, having behavior problems, or dropping out of school related to their academic readiness, motivation, or learning style. This term can also describe students who are learning disabled and struggling English language learners. When we think about assessing them we need to consider several important factors.

One of the most critical factors involved in planning assessments for at-risk students is determining these students' level of social functioning. In addition to academic learning issues, these students can have severe social functioning limitations. They often have weaknesses in impulse control and empathy. In addition, they may have not have developed past the lowest levels of ethical development so that they do not appear to have an intrinsic sense of doing what is right because it is right. They may do what is right if they fear punishment or if they think they will reap a reward. This factor leads many teachers to continue to attach the practice of reward and punishment to their assessments, which may limit students' intrinsic development of ethical behavior.

Activities, such as cooperative learning and partner sharing, can fail if teachers lack classroom management skills and the class is comprised of mostly or all at-risk students. What follows are some possibly useful answers from a book by Belvel and Jordan, *Rethinking Classroom Management* (2003). Based on a study done by the U.S. Department of Labor (Carnevale et al., 1989 as cited in Belvel & Jordan, 2003), Belvel and Jordan propose that students are successful in social activities such as cooperative learning and partner work if they have attained a certain social skill level. Their chart (Belvel & Jordan, 2003, p. 87) includes four levels of social skill development that are necessary for certain kinds of classroom activities (Figure 3.1).

If students show that they are unable to incorporate these social skills in their classroom behaviors, they most likely will not be able to successfully participate in partner or group activities. To remedy this problem, teachers should spend time establishing trusting relationships with these students and also time training them to incorporate these social skills in their own lives. Secondary teachers often resist being teachers of behavior; however, we must realize we are teaching the whole child or young person and that the reality is that many of them have not yet mastered the social skills necessary for these kinds of differentiated assessments. If we wonder why many teachers of at-risk students rely almost exclusively on "worksheets" and "seat work' to assess students' learning, we can understand how this might happen given this information about social skill development. However, just because students might not be "ready" to work with a partner or in a group, does not mean that the teacher should give up on helping to bring those students to a higher level of social performance.

Caution: Students may not show adequate levels of social skill development with one or more teachers, but they may demonstrate these skills with other teachers. Sometimes the only way to tell if a student is truly socially delayed or damaged is if he or she shows social skill deficiency in all classrooms. What may appear to be a student's lack of skills may be a teacher's lack of skills.

Figure 3.1. Levels of Social Skill Development

Level	Description
I. Connecting/bonding skills	1. Knowing other students in the class and calling them by name 2. Making appropriate eye contact with others 3. Treating others with respect 4. Understanding it is important to stay with their group until the teacher tells them to move 5. Understanding it is important to gather and share materials 6. Cleaning up after themselves and their group 7. Solving social problems by asking authorities for help
II. Interacting skills	1. Giving ideas to others 2. Talking about their work 3. Asking relevant questions 4. Saying "Thank you" and other acceptable phrases 5. Including others in decision making 6. Actively listening when others are talking
III. Communicating skills	1. Encouraging others 2. Empathizing 3. Putting their feelings and ideas into their own words 4. Acknowledging the achievements of others 5. Appreciating the input of others 6. Contributing thought ideas to a group or partner discussion
IV. Decision-making and problem-solving skills	1. Listening respectfully to other points of view 2. Generating and implementing thought solutions to identified problems 3. Redirecting the group to work on the task the teacher has assigned 4. Knowing how to use appropriate decision-making strategies 5. Knowing how to summarize for the group

Bevel and Jordan (2003, p. 87) also include a guideline for determine which kinds of social skills might be necessary to do certain kinds of work as shown in Figure 3.2.

Figure 3.2. Work Guidelines

Task	Level II	Level III	Level IV	Level V
Partner work	XXXXXXXX	XXXX		
Small group	XXXXXXXX	XXXXXXXXX	XXXX	
Medium group (larger than 4)	XXXXXXXX	XXXXXXXXX	XXXXXXXXX	XXXX

How to Assess Student Social Functioning

The best way to assess student social functioning is by closely observing them, interviewing them, and surveying them to determine how they rate themselves. In addition to having group and individual conversations with students about their social skills, teachers might use a checklist to give students at the beginning of the year to act as a baseline and a preassessment prior to student attempts to participate in partner or group activities (Figure 3.3).

Figure 3.3. Social Skills Assessment

Answer the following questions true or false.

1. I know the names of most of the students in our class and/or I want to learn their names as soon as possible.   T   F

2. When students talk to me, I look at them and watch their faces.   T   F

3. I respect everyone in the class even if I don't always agree with what they say and do.   T   F

4. I understand and can always follow the rules of the class.   T   F

5. I can work in a group with anybody in this class.   T   F

6. I always clean up after myself.   T   F

7. If someone in my group is messy, I feel it is my responsibility to clean up after them.   T   F

8. I have never had a physical fight with another student.   T   F

9. Everyone in the class, including the teacher, deserves my respect no matter what.   T   F

10. If I have a problem with someone, I can work it out without disrupting the class.   T   F

Many students will not answer this assessment honestly; however, teachers might get a good sense of where the student would like to be if he or she practiced. Teachers might also provide opportunities for peers to evaluate each other, by requiring students to reflect about the behavior of fellow group members. Teachers should evaluate regularly and update assessments at least quarterly. Figure 3.4. is a checklist teachers might use to evaluate students' social skills.

Figure 3.4. Teacher Assessment of Students' Social Skills

Rate each student on the grid below as having ability levels on four important social skills. Give each student a 1 through 4 for each of these four skills.

   1 = no skill; 2 = some skills; 3 = abilities within normal limits; 4 = exceptional ability

   Skill 1: Student is respectful of peers and authority and can empathize with others.

   Skill 2: Student understands how to stay with a group and stay seated until the teacher prompts him or her to move (lacks impulsivity).

   Skill 3: Student solves problems effectively without fighting or disrupting class (lacks impulsivity).

   Skill 4: Student takes appropriate responsibility for doing what is right.

Name	Skill 1	Skill 2	Skill 3	Skill 4	Overall Level & Comments

What is critical here is that teachers realize that so much depends on their own ability to establish a caring relationship based on reasonable expectations and consistency and that they must *teach* at-risk student social skills. *Teachers should not assume that socially challenged students will never be able to work successfully in groups.*

Assessment of At-Risk Students' Attitudes About Success

Key Factors

Assessment of students' experiences and interpretations of a school's (often hidden) curriculum is critical if teachers want to successfully address the needs of at-risk students. These marginalized students experience a lack of belonging in the school and in the world of academic achievement; therefore, to assess their learning, teachers need to also assess their attitudes about and interest in each unit of study. Understanding students' interests and designing assessments that match them helps at-risk students internalize rather than externalize the curriculum and the results of learning (Sagor & Cox, 2004).

It is important for teachers to understand how students *attribute* their success. According to Alderman (1990) there are four different ways:

- Internal/stable—achievement (poor or excellent) comes from inside the student and is consistent (the achiever vs. the loser).

- Internal/unstable—achievement (poor or excellent) comes from inside the student and is not consistent. Student attributes achievement to how much work he or she does.

- External/stable—achievement (poor or excellent) comes from factors outside the student's control and is consistent. Student feels powerless to have any effect on success or failure. Lucky or unlucky.

- External/unstable—achievement (poor or excellent) comes from factors outside the student's control is inconsistent. Student feels that others control his or her success or failure. He or she may attribute success based on how much help the teacher or friend supplies.

See Sagor and Cox (2004) for an extended discussion. Many at-risk students attribute their success to external sources. Teachers should attempt to use differentiated assessment to help at-risk students develop an internal locus of control of their success.

Effects of Teachers' Classroom Management Capabilities and Style on Assessment of At-Risk Students

If teachers do not have the attention and respect of at-risk students in the classroom, they cannot teach them, much less assess their learning. It is a priority, therefore, that teachers pay close attention to the *academic needs* of at-risk students as they affect their management of the classroom. According to Jones and Jones (1990), at-risk students have the following academic needs:

- Understanding the teachers' goals
- Being involved in the learning process
- Relating to the content of the instruction
- Being able to follow their own interests
- Receiving immediate and realistic feedback
- Experiencing success
- Experiencing appropriate structure

- Having time to integrate learning activities

- Having positive contact with peers

- Having instruction that matches their cognitive development and learning styles.

Teachers can develop an assessment tool of their own based on this information or they can use the one from Sagor and Cox (2004, p. 180) to assess the academic needs of at-risk students. If teachers cannot meet these needs, they will most likely experience behavior problems from these students.

Teacher Voices on Using Assessment to Build Relationships with At-Risk Students

Waldo Rogers, who typically has an excellent relationship with students at Lowe's Grove Middle School, says that you cannot teach at-risk students until they like you and trust you. He exemplifies the old saw, "Students don't care what you know until they know that you care." Teachers can use the assessment process to show at-risk students that they care and that they will help them learn.

Don Dixon, who has excellent rapport with *all* of his students, says he builds a "triangle" with his students. The triangle works like this: The teacher loves his subject, the students love the teacher, so the students show that they love the subject the teacher is teaching them by doing well on assessments. After 30 years of teaching, Don Dixon says this triangle has rarely failed him.

Dixon also uses a special classroom management technique based on his belief that the teacher should create the correct atmosphere for learning by creating "high and low points in the lesson." He uses a method he calls "heads down, eyes closed" at strategic points during the lesson. For example, when he senses that students are becoming too loud and chaotic, he will call, "heads down, eyes closed." All students comply with his request, and he is able to redirect them toward more controlled behavior. He also uses this technique if he wants to make sure students are listening carefully to a very short directive. He does not use this method for longer directives because he realizes most of his students need visual as well as auditory cues to attend to and remember what he is asking them to do.

Another idea that will "get at-risk students" on the teacher's side occurs when the teacher has a "desk conference" with the student and discovers that he or she has a good answer to one of the assessment questions. The teacher can call on that student to answer that specific question during class discussion. Helping the at-risk student "look good" goes a long way toward building good relationship with these students through the assessment process.

Planning Effective Assessments for At-Risk Students

When teachers design assessments for at-risk students, they need to keep the following ideas in mind:

- ◆ For any assessment, teachers need to start with questions students can answer without the teacher's help. In other words, teachers need to plan assessments that students can begin independently. If teachers start with difficult ideas or processes, at- risk students may become frustrated, and as a result may act out and disrupt everyone.

- ◆ Teachers should not expect "busy work" to satisfy the needs of at-risk students. They recognize when teachers are giving them work that is too easy.

- ◆ Poorly managed cooperative learning assessments can create problems for at-risk students and can result in what Sagor and Cox (2004) call "sanctioned abandonment" by teachers. As mentioned earlier in this chapter, some of these students may not be socially "ready" for cooperative learning activities. In addition to being socially inept, at-risk students may not do well in some forms of cooperative learning because they tend to leave the work to academically stronger students. The result is that they feel even more left out and inadequate.

- ◆ A quality service-learning project can provide excellent differentiated assessment potential for at-risk students because feeling needed facilitates self-esteem and belonging.

In summary, at-risk students need to see the relevance of assessments. If they cannot see a clear relationship between the assessment and their real world, they will not take the assignment seriously and will not be motivated to achieve. In other words, for at-risk students, teachers should base assessments on authentic standards that have value in the real world. If teachers of at-risk students want to have the best chance for success on assessments, it is critical that they make the following *clear:*

- ◆ Learning objectives, targets, goals
- ◆ Expected performance or product
- ◆ Criteria for evaluation (Sagor & Cox, 2004)

English/Language Arts and Social Studies Examples of Preassessments

Feelings and Beliefs about a Topic

One of the most important things an English language arts teacher might want to preassess is his or her students' attitudes toward reading. Figures 3.5 and 3.6 (following "Procedures") are two surveys that are useful to use with at-risk students.

Procedures

Step 1: Make sure students have a pencil or pen.

Step 2: Hand out the survey to the whole class (see Figure 3.5).

Step 3: Either as a whole class, if all students are at-risk, or to certain clustered students or individuals, have students read the first question aloud, and explain what the question means by giving examples.

Step 4: Ask students to write their response to the first question. Allow enough time by observing when most have finished writing. Do *not* wait for all students to finish writing if you have an extremely slow responder. Keep the pace in line with the majority of the class or you may have trouble from bored students. The slower ones will catch up when it is time for sharing.

Step 5: Ask volunteers to share their responses, and also demand responses until the class has answered all questions.

Figure 3.5. Reading Survey

Please answer the following questions as thoroughly as you can.

1. What strategies do you use when you read? (An example of a reading strategy is rereading when you are not sure what you have read.)

2. How would you describe your reading abilities? (You can use a score of 1–10 with 10 being highest and 1 being lowest.)

3. What role does reading serve in people's personal and public lives? (A role reading might serve in someone's person life is reading a novel for pleasure and a public reason would be to fill out a job application.)

4. What role will reading play in your future education and career goals? (Answer this question by saying what you will be when you grow up and how you will use reading in that job.)

5. List three reading goals you plan to work toward to help you develop as reader. (An example of a reading goal is: "I will improve my ability to read faster this year.")

Survey adapted by S. Waterman based on ideas from *Reading for Understanding: A Guide to Improving Reading in Middle and High School Classrooms; The Reading Apprenticeship Guidebook,* by R. Schoenbach, C. Greenleaf, C. Cziko, & L. Hurwitz, L., 1999, San Francisco, CA: Jossey-Bass and *I Read It, But I Don't Get It: Comprehension Strategies for Adolescent Readers,* by C. Tovani, 2000, Portland, Me: Stenhouse Publishers.

Figure 3.6 shows another way to preassess student interest in reading.

Figure 3.6. Important Book Survey

Name of book:

Author:

Give two reasons you chose this book:

1. _____

2. _____

Respond to these three statements:

1. Describe a specific event or a teacher who helped you feel good about your-self as a reader.

2. Describe a specific event or a teacher that created a problem for you as a reader.

3. Explain how your family has been involved in your growth as a reader.

Adapted by S. Waterman from *Reading for Understanding: A Guide to Improving Reading in Middle and High School Classrooms: The Reading Apprenticeship Guidebook,* by R. Schoenbach, C. Greenleaf, C. Cziko, & L. Hurwitz, 1999, San Francisco, CA: Jossey-Bass; *I Read It, But I Don't Get It: Comprehension Strategies for Adolescent Readers,* by C. Tovani, 2000, Portland, ME: Stenhouse Publishers.

To Scaffold

Teachers should not require at-risk students to complete this assignment for homework. When they present their book to the class, instead of expecting them to present it in the format listed below, the teacher may need to verbally prompt them as follows:

"What is the name of your important book?"

"Who is the author?"

"Can you tell us two reasons you chose that book?"

Then ask them about the book question by question.

Content

Anticipation Guide

What follows is a social studies example of an Anticipation Guide (Herber, 1978). Note that the vocabulary is simple and has ideas at-risk students would be interested in and know something about. In addition, each statement is aligned with the sequence of the text. The way to conduct a lesson using this Anticipation Guide is as follows.

Procedures

Step 1: Hand out the Anticipation Guide as students enter the room.

Step 2: Ask student volunteers or use demand response to have students read each statement out loud. Ask the class to decide if they agree (A) or disagree (D) with the statement. Ask students to raise their hands to indicate agreement or disagreement for each statement. Assure students that if they are wrong, they could actually learn more than if they guess correctly.

Step 3: For the first few statements, walk around the room to make sure all students are putting the A's or D's in the correct box.

Step 4: Go through the statements so that students can indicate agreement or disagreement, and then decide how to read the chapters in the book. Have students take turns reading to find the answers, have pairs read, groups read, or individuals read silently (the least favorite for at-risk students).

Step 5: If students read as a class, it is easy to go over the answers together. Ask students to raise their hands when they think they have found the correct response to the statement.

Step 6: Ask students to read the statement on the Anticipation Guide and then to read the statement in the textbook that proves the statement true or false.

Figure 3.7. Anticipation Guide

Read the statements below and decide if you AGREE (A) or DISAGREE (D) with each statement. Write your answer in the left column under "Anticipate." After you have learned about the topic, complete the right column under "React." Notice what you have learned.

Anticipate	Statement	React	Paragraph Number/ Page Number
	1. In the early and mid 1800s North Carolina was a leader in education.		
	2. Individualism means you are only worried about yourself.		
	3. The invention of the cotton gin by Eli Whitney decreased the need for slaves.		
	4. The economy in a state is how people save money.		
	5. The Trail of Tears was a road from the east to the west.		
	6. Between 1815 and 1850 one-third of the population of North Carolina left to live in other states.		
	7. State leaders used money from the literary fund to buy books for poor children.		
	8. Internal improvements for North Carolina meant building canals and turnpikes.		
	9. School reform in the early to mid 1800s was only for wealthy white children.		
	10. The General Assembly was where students learned about school rules.		
	11. Archibald Murphy felt good about the improvements he made in North Carolina.		

Key: 1. D; 2. A; 3. A; 4. D; 5. D; 6. A; 7. D; 8. A; 9. A; 10. D; 11. D.

Note: Leveled versions of this same Anticipation Guide appear in Chapters 4 and 5.

Note: Don Dixon, a social studies teacher, suggested that one way to adjust this guide is to add a column for page numbers and paragraph numbers, so students may show that they have found the answers in the text. Figure 3.7 (p. 65) shows this adjustment to a typical Anticipation Guide.

Interview Using Accountable Talk

This strategy could cause problems for at-risk students; therefore, teachers should be aware that even though students enjoy interviewing each other, at-risk students may lack the maturity to participate in a meaningful and "on task" conversation.

Procedures

According to Fisher and Frey (2007), at-risk students often lack the skills to participate in academically oriented conversations; therefore, the teacher might use "accountable talk," which is a framework for teaching students how to talk to one another about an academic topic. (See Chapter 2 for details.)

Prior to allowing students to interview one another, the teacher should make sure that they understand accountable talk and are committed to using it. To structure the interview, the teacher should give students an interview template and ask them to find out what at least three other students in the class already know about the topic. They might then turn the template in so that the teacher can get a better idea about what students already know. Students can also take turns sharing what they found out in their interviews. This is a good kinesthetic activity because it gets students moving. Figure 3.8 (p. 67). is a useful template for the interviews.

Figure 3.8. Interview Template

Topic: _____ Your name: _____

Student 1: _____ (name) What he or she thinks about the
topic:_____

_____

_____

_____

_____

_____

_____

_____

Student 2:_____ (name) What he or she thinks about the
topic:_____

_____

_____

_____

_____

_____

_____

_____

Student 3:_____ (name) What he or she thinks about the
topic_____

_____

_____

_____

_____

_____

_____

_____

Informal Assessment

Musical Chairs

Procedures

Latekka Lewis uses an adapted musical chairs activity as a way of informally assessing her students' factual knowledge including understanding of vocabulary terms through a kinesthetic, brain-based method. She follows this process:

Step 1: She picks her music and her questions or vocabulary terms for students to address. The vocabulary terms or questions need to have one right answer so that there is no debate.

Step 2: She does not alter her classroom too much to do this. She merely tells her students to walk around the classroom and when the music stops, they must find a chair. Of course she has removed enough chairs so that one student is always left standing.

Step 3: The student left standing each time must answer the question or define the vocabulary term.

Formative Assessments

Formative assessments allow teachers to determine if their students are learning what the teacher is teaching them. It is assessment *for* learning (Stiggins, Arter, Chappuis, & Chappuis, 2007), not just *of* learning. What follows are several examples of differentiated formative assessment strategies that will help the teacher scaffold assessment for at-risk students.

For each assessment, teachers will see examples of how to address the Differentiating Assessment Template Parts 2 through 5. The first part of the chapter covered Part 1 for all examples, and teachers can only complete Part 6 after they have implemented the assessment. Figure 3.9 is a review of the template for this process.

Figure 3.9. Differentiating Assessment: Six-Part Template

1. Students' Needs (described in detail)				
2. Curriculum				
Standard Course of Study (SCOS)	Essential Question (EQ)	Know	Understand	Do *(See MO below)*
3. Measurable Objective (MO)				
Introduction	Thinking Verb(s)	Product	Response Criterion	Content
4. Differentiation				
Readiness		Interests		Learning Styles
5. Assessment Procedures (listed by steps)				
6. Assessment Audit				

Examples of Formative Assessments

Differentiated Formative Assessments by Learning Styles

For the assessment strategies that follow, I use the differentiated and strategic categorizations discussed in Silver, Strong, and Perini (2007): mastery, understanding, self-expression, interpersonal, and four-style. I have adapted (including using alternative names for some similar concepts) their descriptions of these best practices, and I have focused on structuring the aspect of their usefulness as English and social studies assessment strategies for at-risk students.

Mastery-Based Assessments

New American Lecture

Teachers can use this method (adapted from Ausubel, 1963, 1968; Silver, Strong, & Perini, 2007) of assessing using an interactive PowerPoint presentation (Figure 3.10). The main idea with this strategy is to construct a lesson that provides a small amount of information and then stopping to ask students to respond to questions that require different styles of thought to synthesize their learning. It is important to give at-risk students plenty of time to record their answers to questions or other types of prompts on a sheet of paper, and then to allow them to share their answers.

Figure 3.10. New American Lecture

Curriculum				
SCOS	**EQ:** What is the culture of our Hispanic neighbors and immigrants?	**Know**—information about ancient Latin America and how to participate in an interactive presentation	**Understand** that learning about ancient Latin America helps us understand the culture of our Hispanic neighbors and immigrants	**Do**—think, write, and share ideas inspired by a lecture on ancient Latin America *(see MO below)*

Measurable Objective				
Introduction	**Thinking Verb(s)**	**Product**	**Response Criterion**	**Content**
Students will…	exemplify, generate, and classify in order to produce	short written and spoken answers	that answer the questions prompted by the PowerPoint presentation	about ancient Latin America.

Differentiation		
Readiness—teacher uses brain-based ideas to present information in an interactive lecture	**Interests**—this is an engaging process that allows students to interact with a teachers' presentation	**Style**—interpersonal, visual, verbal/linguistic, mastery

Procedures

Figure 3.11 is an outline of information that teachers might use with the whole class as a PowerPoint presentation that includes graphics. Note that teachers should stop to assess students' learning during and after each slide. For at-risk students teachers can increase students' interaction by leaving out words in the text to encourage engagement in the presentation. The italicized words are those that the students should supply. This assessment includes oral, informal methods, but it also requires that students hand in written work that teachers will evaluate.

Figure 3.11. Social Studies New American Lecture—PowerPoint Presentation

---

Slide 1

Ancient Latin America

What is happening in this picture?

(Show a picture of a cultural event taking place in a Latin American country.)

Three Major Ancient Latin American Cultures

- ◆ The Maya

- ◆ The Aztec

- ◆ The Inca

Slide 1 Explanation: Tell students that they will be exploring three major ancient Latin American cultures, and after they have described what they think is going on in the picture, ask them to explain what they already know about these cultures. Find out if any students come from any of these three cultures.

Slide 2

The Maya

What is happening in this picture?

(Show a colorful graphic of the area which made up the ancient Mayan culture.)

Where is this?

The *Maya* lived in Mexico and Central America.

Slide 2 Explanation: While showing this slide teachers should talk about where this culture thrived in relationship to other parts of the Americas and in the world. Teachers could encourage students to find it on a world map. Make sure students can fill in the blank at the bottom of the slide.

Slide 3

The Maya

What is happening in this picture?

(Show a picture from the ancient Mayan culture.)

When did it exist?

Small communities existed from as early as 1600 BC until AD 900.

They established one of Latin America's most
important and long-lasting *cultures*.

Slide 3 Explanation: Focus on how long ago this culture existed. Encourage students to determine the total number of years this culture lasted.

Slide 4

The Maya

What is happening in this picture?

*(Show a picture related to early Mayan
mathematics and astronomy.)*

They studied *mathematics* and astronomy and were one of the
first civilizations in the world to understand the advanced mathematical concept of zero.

Slide 4 Explanation: This slide provides an excellent opportunity to make connections with mathematics and science and to admire Hispanic culture for its part in advancing mathematical and scientific concepts.

Slide 5

The Maya

(Show pictures of one or more of the Mayan calendars.)

They had three complex *calendars*.

Slide 5 Explanation: Use this slide to encourage students to compare and contrast these calendars with our modern day one.

Slide 6

The Maya

(Show a picture of Mayan glyphs.)

They established the most well-developed written language
in ancient Latin America.

The writing system using symbols (glyphs) is called *glyphic*.

Slide 6 Explanation: Teachers may need to write the word *glyphic* so that students can spell it. This slide provides another opportunity to compare and contrast ancient written language with our modern way of writing. Stress that not all ancient cultures developed writing and discuss the importance of being able to write.

Slide 7

The Maya

(Show a picture of slash-and-burn farming.)

The Maya used slash-and-burn *farming*: cutting down and burning
trees to plant crops in their place.

Slide 7 Explanation: Ask students to evaluate this kind of farming in terms of use of natural resources. Ask them to think about why the Mayans used this method.

Slide 8

The Maya Decline

(Show a picture of a Mayan ruin.)

Around 900 A.D. things began to change. Building
stopped, and people left the cities.

What do you think happened?

Write your ideas. Share.

Slide 8 Explanation: Allow students to share their ideas about why the culture declined.

Slide 9

The Maya

(Show a picture of modern-day people of Mayan ancestry.)

More than 6 _million_ Mayan people now live in Guatemala, Belize, and Southern Mexico.

Slide 9 Explanation: Focus on what we might learn from our ancestors and how we might use that knowledge in our present lives.

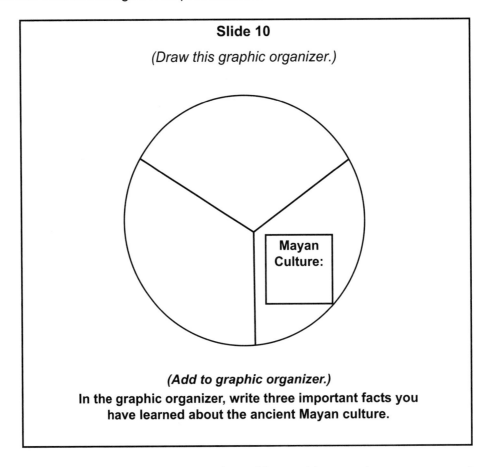

Slide 10

(Draw this graphic organizer.)

Mayan Culture:

(Add to graphic organizer.)
**In the graphic organizer, write three important facts you
have learned about the ancient Mayan culture.**

Slide 10 Explanation: Ask students to draw this graphic organizer on a separate piece of paper and to add three facts about the Mayan culture in one of the three sections.

Continue this PowerPoint presentation in a similar fashion discussing the Aztec and the Incas.

Note—Fair Use Slide: If teachers use this outline to construct a PowerPoint presentation with accompanying pictures, they need to remember to credit sources and include a "fair use" statement at the end of the PowerPoint presentation.

Understanding-Based Formative Assessments

Compare and Contrast

Using graphic organizers to show how various concepts and ideas are similar and different can help at-risk students improve their higher-order thinking ability. Figure 3.12 (p. 76) provides an example of a compare and contrast assessment (adapted from Marzano et al., 2001).

Procedures

The strategy includes four phases for students: (1) observe or read, (2) compare using a graphic organizer (Figure 3.13, p. 77), (3) draw conclusions about comparisons, and (4) summarize learning about comparisons. The teacher can note achievement at phases 2 through 4.

To scaffold this assignment, include a text that students can read independently and silently (the Internet is a good resource), or if you cannot find that kind of text, you might use a shared reading strategy that allows all students access to the text. Show students how to fill out at least one line in "Similarities" and one in "Differences."

Figure 3.12. Compare and Contrast

Curriculum				
SCOS	**EQ:** What are the differences between democracy and monarchy?	**Know**—similarities and differences between democracy and monarchy	**Understand** that knowing the similarities and differences between democracy and monarchy help deepen our understanding of the actions of government	**Do**—determine similarities and differences between democracy and monarchy *(see MO below)*

Measurable Objective				
Introduction	**Thinking Verb(s)**	**Product**	**Response Criterion**	**Content**
Students will…	generate, and compare	using a Venn diagram	and include at least three differences and three similarities	between democracy and monarchy.

Differentiation		
Readiness—graphic organizer provided by the teacher scaffolds the assessment	**Interests**—students note ideas that interest them	**Style**—understanding, visual, investigative

**Figure 3.13. Similarities and Differences Graphic Organizer—
Social Studies Example**

**As you read the chapters, complete this organizer.
What is being compared and contrasted?**

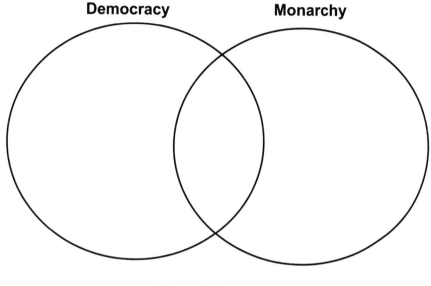

Democracy   Monarchy

Venn Diagram

Self-Expression–Based Formative Assessments

Inductive Learning with Picture Books

This is a brainstorming and predicting process that includes grouping, labeling, and generalizing to construct essential ideas. It is a wonderful assessment strategy to use if teachers want students to practice using inductive reasoning. At-risk students can truly enjoy this process because it does not have to include very much reading and writing, which often denies them access to learning activities. Figure 3.14 (p. 78) is an English/language arts example of an inductive learning assessment strategy. It is adapted from the work of Taba (1971) and Silver, Strong, and Perini (2007).

Figure 3.14. Inductive Learning

Curriculum				
SCOS	**EQ:** How do certain picture books exemplify certain text structures? How can we use the process of inductive reasoning to generalize about text structures?	**Know**—how to construct generalizations about various picture books through an inductive process.	**Understand** that we can use an inductive process to generalize about the text structure of a picture book.	**Do**—visit learning centers that have picture books, choose text structures from a list, use induction to generalize text structures in picture books *(see MO below)*.

Measurable Objective				
Introduction	**Thinking Verb(s)**	**Product**	**Response Criterion**	**Content**
Students will…	compare, explain, generate, attribute, critique in order to produce	a completed graphic organizer that includes generalizations and evaluations	that are accurate and sufficient	about the text structure of six picture books.

Differentiation		
Readiness—teacher-led process and experiential learning activities scaffold assessment	**Interests**—a variety of interesting picture books will capture students' attention	**Style**—self-expression, visual, investigative, kinesthetic

Procedures

Step 1: Set up mini-assessment stations (learning stations) that each have a picture book representing a specific literary style. For at-risk students the number of mini-assessment stations should allow no more than four students to experience the station at one time.

Step 2: Give each student a booklet of graphic organizers that will guide his or her experiences in the mini stations. The graphic organizer could look like Figure 3.15.

Figure 3.15. Graphic Organizer

Title of Book:
Author:
Write two to three sentences explaining what the book is about.   _____   _____   _____
State the story text structure:
Explain in one to two sentences generalizing about that structure: _____   _____
Evaluate the book (1 is lowest and 10 is highest)   1   2   3   4   5   6   7   8   9   10
Write one to three sentences explaining why you gave the book that rating.   _____   _____   _____

Step 3: Each learning station will have a picture book that represents a text structure. Direct students to take turns reading the book and choosing from a list of text structures shown in the Figure 3.16 handout to generalize about which structure the book represents. Students can collaborate, but each student must complete his or her own booklet of graphic organizers.

Figure 3.16. Text Structures

Text Structures

Choose from this list to generalize about the text structure for each picture book.

- Repeated, wraparound paragraph text
- Handbook or guide text
- Narrative sequenced by a series of objects, people, or animals
- Circular text
- Story within a story
- Narrative poem text

Book Titles

1. *My Mama Had a Dancing Heart* (1995) by Libby Moore Gray
2. *Everglades* (1995) by Jean Craighead George
3. *Nathaniel Talking* (1988) by Eloise Greenfield
4. *The Pirate's Handbook: How to Become a Rogue of the High Seas* (1995) by Margaret Lincoln
5. *Raven and River* (1997) by Nancy White Carlstrom
6. *So Much!* (1994) by Trish Cook

Key: 1. Circular text; 2. Story within a story; 3. Narrative poem text; 4. Handbook or guide text; 5. Repeated, wraparound paragraph text; 6. Narrative sequenced by a series of objects, people, or animals.

Step 4: Evaluate the student booklets and then have a class discussion. An assignment to demonstrate further evidence of learning could be that students write in a style they or you chose.

Many of the ideas for this assessment come from Katie Wood Ray's wonderful book, *Wondrous Words: Writers and Writing in the Elementary Classroom* (1999). Even though this book is primarily for elementary grades, it has many helpful ideas for secondary teachers.

Interpersonal-Based Assessments

Interpersonal-based assessments use students' natural inclination to help each other and work together; however, with at-risk students, these kinds of activities can be tricky if the teacher does not feel that students are ready for them. If teachers are closely monitoring student social skill level, they may conclude that most, but not all of the students can participate in these kinds of assessments. If some students cannot be successful working with others, teachers should consider assigning them to do the work on their own. What follows are some interpersonal-based assessment strategies that include ways to prepare at-risk students to participate in them.

Problem Solving Using a Decision-Making Model

This is an interesting way to get students personally involved in a topic so that they feel some ownership about it and care about it. It is an adaptation from Silver, Strong, and Perini (2007). Caring about a topic is especially important as a motivating factor for at-risk students; however, because they need extra structure to complete interpersonal and higher-level thinking activities such as group decision making, teachers often leave out these kinds of assessments. Teachers might choose a topic about which they know students are passionate. They can guide students toward social studies or English-related topics by showing a PowerPoint presentation that piques their interest or reading an article in a magazine or newspaper that is social studies or English-based and relevant to students' lives. Figure 3.17 is a social studies example in which at-risk students might explore what to do about "drought." Note that teachers can easily integrate this assessment with science and English.

Figure 3.17. Problem Solving—"Drought"

Curriculum				
SCOS	**EQ:** How can we use the six-step problem-solving method to deal with a serious community issue such as drought?	**Know**—how to use the six-step problem-solving method to plan solutions to the problem of drought.	**Understand** that the six-step problem-solving method helps us deal with serious community issues such as drought.	**Do**—use the six-step problem-solving method to find ways to solve the problem of drought *(see MO below)*.

Measurable Objective				
Introduction	**Thinking Verb(s)**	**Product**	**Response Criterion**	**Content**
Students will…	compare, implement, differentiate, critique, and produce	data and a plan	that leads to an efficient way to solve	the problem of drought in a community.

Differentiation		
Readiness—teacher-led process, with structured practice, graphic organizers scaffolds assessment	**Interests**—working on a real community problem	**Style**—interpersonal, visual, creative

Procedures

The Drought Project

Assuming that students have identified drought as the primary topic of interest, proceed in a whole-class activity (not in small groups) to begin the six-step problem-solving process in template form to help guide at-risk students through the process.

Record students' ideas as the whole class discusses each of these steps together. Write the answers on an overhead version or type the answers in a projected version of this template. For at-risk students it is important that they can see what to write as well as hear what to write. Figure 3.18 shows the six steps and Figure 3.19 is a template.

Figure 3.18. Six-Step Problem Solving

Step 1: What are the problems and challenges associated with the lack of adequate water? Answers could include: can't use the toilet, can't take a bath, can't wash clothes, can't brush teeth, can't have school, can't go out to eat, can't water plants, etc. What are the challenges involved in solving the problem of lack of adequate water? (Notice how these questions are different and will elicit a different style of answer.)

Answers: People waste too much water, government leaders are not finding more water, people are greedy about their own needs for water, we don't know how to save water, and government is not doing enough about global warming.

Step 2: The class decides which of the statements about challenges (or a combination of statements) if solved would do the most to solve the problem.

Help the students construct a statement that includes a condition statement, a key verb phrase, what should happen, and under what circumstances it should happen. An example of this kind of statement is, "Our community has been experiencing a drought that has made us worry about having enough water to be comfortable. How might we conserve the water resources in our community so that if we have more droughts we will not have to worry about not having enough water."

Step 3: Each student thinks of at least one thing a group of students could do to solve the challenge. Students record their solution idea, but make sure they record the five solutions that the class generates.

Solutions could be as follows:

1. Make brochures with water conservation tips.
2. Make containers for people to collect rain water.
3. Make posters with water conservation tips.
4. Make commercials that publicize the need to conserve water.
5. Write letters to the newspaper to encourage people to conserve water.

Step 4: Use the following criteria to evaluate each of the five solutions:

Criterion 1: Which solution costs the least amount of money?

Criterion 2: Which solution takes the least amount of time to create?

Criterion 3: Which solution would reach the most people?

Criterion 4: Which solution would have the fewest roadblocks?

Criterion 5: Which solution would be the most fun for the students to do?

Step 5: Use the following chart to evaluate each of the solutions for each of the criteria. Do this as a class.

Solutions	C1	C2	C3	C4	C5	Totals
Suggestion1: Make brochures	3	2	2	4	3	14
Suggestion 2: Containers to collect rain	2	4	1	3	2	12
Suggestion 3: Make posters	4	5	3	5	4	21
Suggestion 4: Make commercials	1	3	5	2	5	16
Suggestion 5: Write articles for newspaper	5	1	4	1	1	12

Rate each criteria by numbering it 1, 2, 3, 4, or 5; 5 is highest, and 1 is lowest. Add up the numbers and note the solution that gets the most points. See examples above. Do one criteria at a time and try not to give a score more than once.

Step 6: Students make a plan for making posters because that solution received the highest score. They include who will do what, where and how they will get their information, and other specifics. Each student should write his own plan, and then share it with the class. Notice that at no point do students work together. When they actually implement the plan, they might work in groups, but not before. Students could actually make posters individually, with a partner or in a small group. The teacher could have them printed for distribution. Or the teacher could hold a poster making contest.

Figure 3.19. Template for Six-Step Problem Solving

Step 1: What are the problems and challenges associated with the lack of adequate water?

What are the challenges involved in solving the problem of lack of adequate water?

Step 2: Write the statement the class decides is the critical issue that if it is solved would make the most difference.

Step 3: Write at lease one solution that addresses the critical issue stated above.

Write the five solutions the class generates:
1. _____
2. _____
3. _____
4. _____
5. _____

Step 4: Use the following criteria to evaluate each of the five solutions:
Criterion 1: Which solution costs the least amount of money?
Criterion 2: Which solution takes the least amount of time to create?
Criterion 3: Which solution would reach the most people?
Criterion 4: Which solution would have the fewest roadblocks?
Criterion 5: Which solution would be the most fun for the students to do?
You may offer alternative criteria if you wish.

Step 5: Use the following chart to evaluate each of the solutions for each of the criteria. Do this as a class.

Solutions	C1	C2	C3	C4	C5	Totals
1.						
2.						
3.						
4.						
5.						

Put a number 1, 2, 3, 4, or 5 for each of the criteria; 5 is highest, and 1 is lowest. Add up the numbers and note the solution that gets the most points. Do one criterion at a time and try not to give a score more than once.

Step 6: Write a plan for making posters. Include how you would gather information, who would do what, when you would make them. Share your plan with the class.

Four-Style Assessment

Seminar, Socratic Seminar, Circle of Knowledge

This is a method of assessing students orally. It is adapted from Silver, Strong, and Perini (2007). It can be ineffective and counterproductive for at-risk students because most of them are eager to share their thoughts and feelings, but they can become abusive with one another, and they can take a discussion completely out of an academic realm. This is not to say that these students should not have opportunities to share their feelings, thoughts, and values, such as in classroom meetings; however, for assessment purposes this kind of assessment is best "tied to a text." For at-risk students, it is important to start slowly and increase the time in circles as students improve their skills. Figure 3.20 (p. 86) is an example of a seminar experience for at-risk students, starting with a process useful to both English and social studies and finishing with an English/social studies example.

Procedures

Seminar Assessment—General and English Example

Step 1: Identify a relatively simple text for the students' first experience with seminar. This text should be broken up with graphics or pictures and should have short paragraphs. Ask students to read this selection and annotate it as best they can (meaning making notes on the side with questions and other ideas). For extremely low-performing students, you can choose to read and annotate the selection as a whole-class activity.

Step 2: Tell students that during the next class, they will be participating in a seminar discussion of this text and that everyone should bring at least two questions to help with the discussion. At-risk students like to feel that they have some control and input into what happens in class; therefore, allowing them to write questions is motivational.

How to Write Seminar Questions

Teach students to write Level 2 and 3 type questions. Explain that a Level 1 question has one answer, so that it would not be an appropriate "discussion" question, and then model for them how to construct a Level 2 question (one that the person answering must infer and that can have many answers) based on the text they have just read. Walk around the room and have mini desk conferences to make sure each student knows how to write this kind of question. Next, teach them how to write a Level 3 question, which uses the text as a base but moves beyond it into themes. For at-risk students, provide this stem to get them started on this question

Figure 3.20. Seminar

Curriculum				
SCOS	**EQ:** What does the book, *Anne Frank: The Dairy of a Young Girl,* teach us about religious and racial oppression and self-sacrifice?	**Know**—how to successfully discuss *Anne Frank: The Dairy of a Young Girl* in a seminar session, how to follow the rules of seminar, how to make and support claims.	**Understand** that the book, *Anne Frank: The Dairy of a Young Girl* teaches us many important concepts such as the horror of religious and racial oppression and self-sacrifice.	**Do**—ask and answer important questions about a literary work *(see MO below).*

Measurable Objective				
Introduction	**Thinking Verb(s)**	**Product**	**Response Criterion**	**Content**
Students will…	explain, summarize, produce, exemplify, attribute, and generate	oral responses	that are respectful of others, thorough, accurate, and reference the text	about the book, *Anne Frank: The Dairy of a Young Girl.*

Differentiation		
Readiness—teacher-led process and practice scaffolds assessment	**Interests**—students think of their own questions and answers for a highly interesting topic	**Style**—interpersonal, mastery, understanding, and self-expression, verbal/linguistic, auditory

level: "What does this text (specify the title of the selection) teach us about…? (Model for them how they might supply a theme idea such asjustice, responsibility, violence, etc.) Check that each student has successfully written a Level 3 question. Tell students that their "ticket to seminar is two discussion questions about the text." Make sure each student has written these questions before they leave class; you can even collect them so that they will be available for the next class.

Step 3: For the next class, arrange the desks in a circle. Some teachers can be terrified of moving their desks out of rows, especially for at-risk students, because teachers lose some control when they do not have all eyes facing forward and centered on them. You might want to gradually move into circles by first arranging desks as shown in Figure 3.21.

Figure 3.21. Desks Arranged in "Precircle" Configuration

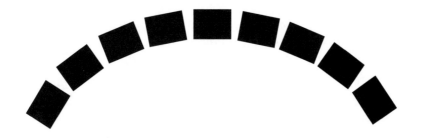

Assigning seats ahead of time is the best practice to ward off side conversations between friends. The best way to assign seats is to have a picture of the circle posted with a reference point (a desk, window, or door) to show where the circle starts.

Step 4: At-risk students, who may not have experienced a discussion group in a circle, may be somewhat agitated; therefore, allow some settle-down time and provide some friendly assurance that students are going to enjoy this activity.

Step 5: Join the circle and explain the rules and expectations that you have posted in the room. Another idea is to hand out a copy of the rules and expectations to students in addition to posting them. The best rules and expectations for at-risk students are in Figure 3.22.

Figure 3.22. Seminar Rules and Expectations

1. Be respectful of everyone. *(Seminar is a great chance for at-risk students to practice this social skill. For those students who cannot or will not be respectful for this process, provide an alternative assignment for them. Make sure students understand that monopolizing the group by answering all or most of the questions is a form of disrespect. You can penalize students in some way including lowering their grades for seminar if they monopolize the discussion.)*

2. You do not need to raise your hand to speak. *(This is important because the discussion should be student-controlled, and if students raise their hands, the teacher stays in control.)*

3. Keep your eyes on the person who is speaking. *(This is important because students will not know when the speaker has finished, and they may begin speaking. It is also the respectful thing to do.)*

4. Group conversations only. *(You can head off this problem by assigning seats in advance.)*

5. Reference the text. *(Make sure students understand how to help others see their references by making sure everyone knows how to start with page numbers and then identify the correct paragraph.)*

6. Use standard English. *(Because this process is an oral assessment, hold students accountable to the same standards of correct English to which you hold them for a written assignment.)*

For each of these rules and expectations, stop and ask students to explain why this rule is important and model what it would look like as it is experienced. *This is critical* to the success of a seminar with at-risk students. As the seminar proceeds gently remind students to follow the correct procedures. Here are some good phrases to use that are successful with at-risk students:

♦ "Standard English, please."
♦ "You don't have to raise your hand, just speak out."
♦ "Can you reference the text?"
♦ "Help us find the words you are reading."

Step 6: To finish seminar, give shy or reluctant students a chance to speak. Give these students a "parting shot" question that is relatively easy to answer. To grade a seminar, use the oral assessment grading grid shown in Chapter 2. Figure 3.23 provides an English seminar example.

Figure 3.23. English Example of Seminar

Step 1: Ask students to read *Anne Frank: The Diary of a Young Girl.* Note: For at-risk students, teachers may need to teach this book chapter by chapter prior to assessing students' understanding of it.

Step 2: Explain how to write Level 2 and 3 questions. Here are some Level 2 examples for this topic:

- ◆ Which character is most like you in terms of personality?
- ◆ What event caused the most suspense in the story?
- ◆ How did the families manage to get along through the ordeal of hiding together?
- ◆ Why is it important that Anne Frank wrote a diary?

Here are some Level 3 examples:

- ◆ What does *Anne Frank: The Diary of a Young Girl* teach us about responsibility?
- ◆ Why is *Anne Frank: The Diary of a Young Girl* an important work?
- ◆ How do the themes in *Anne Frank: The Diary of a Young Girl* affect the school community?
- ◆ What might *Anne Frank: The Diary of a Young Girl* teach us about injustice?

Follow the general rules and expectations for the remainder of this process.

With all of these formative assessments, it is important to rotate them so that students have an opportunity to experience each type of assessment.

Summative Assessments for At-Risk Students

Most textbooks provide summative assessments for teachers to use; however, for at-risk students, *it might be best for teachers to create their own unit tests based on their standard course of study and based on student needs.* To construct a "fair" summative assessment for at-risk students, teachers might evaluate their assessment based on the checklists in Chapter 2.

Constructing Summative Assessments for At-Risk Students

True/False Tests

True/false questions are problematic because of guessing, which at-risk students are accustomed to doing. One way to solve this problem is to require students to correct statements they believe are false. Figure 3.24 (p. 90) shows true/false question examples for English and social studies.

Figure 3.24. True/False Question Examples

English

1. A subordinate clause is a group of words that can stand alone.

2. Autobiography is a literary work written by a person about himself or herself.

Key: 1. F—It is a group of words that cannot stand alone; it needs to be attached to an independent clause or it is a sentence fragment; 2. T

Social Studies

1. The most populous country is China.

2. According to the *Declaration of the Rights of Man and of the Citizen* (1789), the right that belongs to all people is the right to choose their government.

Key: 1. T; 2. F—All people according to this document have the right to liberty, property, security, and resistance to oppression.

Short Answer

The following is a description of a social studies example of a short-answer discussion test that is fair to at-risk students because it is "student-friendly." Teachers can find pictures on the Internet to use for these short-answer tests. They should credit their sources.

Figure 3.25. Social Studies Short Answer

Social Studies Short Answer Test

Name: _____ Date: _____

1. How is slavery an example of oppression?

    (Include a picture that represents slavery.)

2. List 4 effects of the invention of the cotton gin?

    (Include a picture of the cotton gin.)

3. Explain the similarities and differences between the slaves from the country and slaves from the city.

    (Include a picture from the country or city during the 1800's)

4. What effect did religion have on slavery?

    (Include a religious symbol.)

5. Explain the similarities and differences between Fredrick Douglass and Nat Turner.

   (Include a picture of either of these men or both of them.)

Note: Pictures for your test are easy to find using Google Images.

Key: Answers might be some of the following:

1. Oppression is one person or group of people dominating another person or group of people. Slavery is an example of oppression because one group of people owned and had total control over another person or group of people. Any time a person does not have free will, they are victims of oppression.

2. The 4 effects of the invention of the cotton gin are as follows: 1. more people moved west and anywhere the weather made it possible to grow cotton, 2. famers grew more cotton than any other crop and exported more of it, 3. more Native Americans were pushed off their land, 4. slavery expanded in the south and west.

3. Slaves in the country did field work, but salves in the cities worked as day laborers, craftsmen, and domestic workers.

4. White ministers used biblical passages that encouraged slaves to serve their masters, and African Americans used those that showed how God freed slaves.

5. Both rebelled against slavery. Fredrick Douglass did so peacefully and through writing and speaking to the public, but Nat Turner did so by killing his masters and other whites.

Multiple Choice

Most textbooks include the capability to construct multiple-choice tests for students; however, for at-risk students, it is best that teachers construct their own tests. It might even help these students if teachers teach them how to write questions with appropriate distracters.

The best kinds of distracters fall into one of these categories: misconception, oversimplification, or overgeneralization. Figure 3.26 is a social studies example of a multiple-choice question that exemplifies each of these types of distracters.

Figure 3.26. Social Studies Example: Analyzing Distracters

1. Which of these statements *best* describes the Boston Tea Party?
   A. The Boston Tea Party was the only event in which colonists destroyed tea to protest taxation without representation. (misconception)
   B. The Boston Tea Party made the British very angry. (oversimplification)
   C. The Boston Tea Party was a major cause of the Revolutionary War. (overgeneralization)
   D. The Boston Tea Party was an event in which colonists destroyed more than 300 chests of tea to protest taxation without representation. (correct answer)

Extended-Writing Response

Figure 3.27 shows some extended writing prompts for English and social studies. Notice that the prompts are short and to the point because at-risk students may have trouble with longer prompts.

Figure 3.27 Extended-Writing Prompts

English Essay Prompts for At-Risk Students

1. Explain why you love or hate studying literature.
2. If you were in charge of the school, would you make everyone take English classes? Why or why not?
3. During this course, you have learned about how a setting might affect the plot or theme of a piece of literature. Explain in two strong paragraphs (about seven sentences each), how the setting might affect the plot or theme of a story or novel you have read this year or in the past.
4. Choose a story or novel you have read and explain three ways one of the characters in that story or novel is like you.
5. Write a letter to your best friend recommending your favorite book or movie. Make sure to include at least two good reasons why you recommend the book or movie.
6. What is the worst problem at your school? Write an article for your school newspaper explaining the problem and offering a way to solve it.

Social Studies Essay Prompts for At-Risk Students

1. Think of an important historical event and explain in a five-paragraph essay the effects of that event on our lives today. You must think of at least three effects.
2. Think of an important social problem experienced by teens and explain how a teacher or counselor might help solve it.
3. Explain the effects of a failing economy on those who live in public housing.

4. Explain the most important cause or effect of slavery on the cultural identities of African Americans.

5. Which period in history is the most interesting to you? Why?

For at-risk students, it is important that teachers help them plan their extended writing response using a writing planner (graphic organizer). Teachers may actually look at the plan first to determine if students are on the right track before they take time writing a response. Figure 3.28 is a suggested generic graphic organizer for expository (nonfiction) writing including persuasion.

Figure 3.28. Generic Writing Planner

Paragraph 1
◆ Lead (an interesting beginning to the essay):
◆ Thesis (reflects the prompt):
◆ Summary of main points:
Paragraph 2
◆ Topic sentence or main idea:
◆ Supporting details (include at least three examples or elaborations)
◆ So what? (includes conclusions you might draw based on your ideas)
Paragraph 3
◆ Topic sentence or main idea.
◆ Supporting details (include at least three examples or elaborations)
◆ So what? (includes conclusions you might draw based on your ideas)
Paragraph 4
◆ Topic sentence or main idea.
◆ Supporting details (include at least three examples or elaborations)
◆ So what? (includes conclusions you might draw based on your ideas)
Paragraph 5
◆ Restated thesis:
◆ Summary of main ideas:
◆ Parting comment (should be a powerful ending):

Projects and Performances

At-risk student do not typically have many opportunities to show what they know through projects. Figures 3.29 and 3.30 provide examples of projects that work well with at-risk students.

Figure 3.29. English Project

A Mouse Journal

This is a great assessment to use with at-risk students if the teacher has assigned a challenging book for the whole class to read together. The teacher can assign students to keep a "Mouse Journal."

Procedures

Materials: colored construction paper cut in small rectangles and folded over (see approximate exact size below), pieces of lined paper cut to fit the folded over construction paper; markers, crayons, or colored pencils. Help students staple the lined paper into the cover.

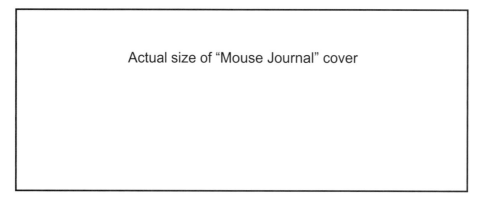

Actual size of "Mouse Journal" cover

Step 1: Tell the class that they are going to make a "Mouse Journal" as a project associated with the novel they are reading. Tell them that the journal is small like a mouse so that they must write small and shorten the story so that it will fit into a small book.

Step 2: Ask students to create a mouse character who will tell the story that is going on in the novel. This mouse should have a distinct personality, and he or she will be watching the action and commenting on it as an omniscient being.

Step 3: Provide the materials listed above and give students time to create their mouse journals. Inform students that after they finish reading each chapter of the novel their "mouse" should write an entry into the journal. Note: *You may need to teach, reteach, or review the process of summarizing information prior to expecting students to be successful doing this project.*

Step 4: Students will share their journals after each chapter. Check that students are reading the novel accurately. This activity allows you to keep track of students' comprehension of the novel as they read rather than at the end of the process. Each journal entry is a summative evaluation of students' understanding and compliance with the directive to read a certain amount of pages before each class.

Step 5: The final project could be a Journal Reading Event to which parents might be invited.

I created this project idea and have used it with *The Odyssey* and with *Anne Frank: The Dairy of a Young Girl*. It gives students a great chance to be creative while also holding them accountable for understanding the work.

If you want at-risk students to have fun with a topic in social studies, assess learning by asking them to create a newsletter that shows what they have learned about that topic (Figure 3.30). Figure 3.31 explains how to conduct the research for the newsletter and Figure 3.32 (p. 96) is a possible syllabus and *checklist evaluation* for this kind of project.

Figure 3.30. Social Studies Project

Newsletter

Procedures

Step 1: Ask students to choose a topic from a recent unit or assign them a topic.

Step 2: Show students how to use a "newsletter" generating program on a computer. (I use Microsoft Office Publisher.)

Step 3: Instruct, reteach, or review with students how to use research to inform their projects. Review the "Big 6" (see Figure 3.31) method of research and directly instruct students in research methods (including how to cite sources) as they work on these newsletters.

Figure 3.31. Big Six Steps for Conducting Research

I. Task Definition
- *Read* relevant background information about the topic.
- Write a *state*ment or question that clearly identifies the information needed to adequately address the topic.
- Accurately *define* the topic using key word phrases.
- *Identify* the information requirements for the topic (Acceptable resources, how many? Types? How current? Level of author's authority on the subject?).
- List tasks in order and *create* a schedule for accomplishing them.

II. Information-Seeking Strategies
- *List the range of possible sources* you know of and can use (primary and secondary, hard copy and online).
- *Ask* another person to help you identify sources.
- *Evaluate* different possible sources to determine priorities.

III. Location and Access

 ♦ *Locate* sources and determine if they are in the school media center, in the community library, in the classroom, or at home (primary and secondary, online and hard copy).

 ♦ *Find* information in hard-copy sources using a table of contents, glossary, or index.

 ♦ *Find* information in online sources by conducting word and subject searches.

IV. Use of Information

 ♦ *Read, hear, or view* the information from a source to note main ideas and other dates that might be useful for your product.

 ♦ *Evaluate* the accuracy and validity of the information in a source.

 ♦ *Gather* information from various sources.

 ♦ *Collect* all appropriate information from sources to cite them correctly in the paper.

V. Synthesis

 ♦ *Develop* an outline.

 ♦ Put note cards from multiple sources in correct *order*. Cite sources on a Works Cited page.

 ♦ *Organize* research findings effectively.

 ♦ Present research finding in a well-constructed paper.

VI. Evaluation

 ♦ *Decide* if the project is complete and satisfies the requirements of the assignment (e.g., checking the rubric)

 ♦ Learn from mistakes and do a better job in the future.

From *Information Problem Solving: The Big Six*. Accessed December 3, 2005 at http://www.jlhs.nhusd.k12.ca.us/Classes/Science/Research.html.

Figure 3.32. Syllabus for Research-Based Newsletter Project

1.	Choose a relevant topic from our unit of study.	(5 points)	___Yes	___No
2.	Create a four-page newsletter about that topic.	(20 points)	___Yes	___No
3.	Use interesting graphics and layout.	(20 points)	___Yes	___No
4.	Include information that sufficiently and accurately covers the topic you have chosen.	(30 points)	___Yes	___No
5.	Include at least three sources of information. Cite your sources correctly using MLA style.	(15 points)	___Yes	___No
6.	Review your work to look for misspelled words and grammar errors.	(10 points)	___Yes	___No

7. Save your work and print a hard copy of it.

8. Turn in the newsletter by_____.

Points deducted:_____   Reason:

Total points earned:_____

Grade:_____

Teacher comments:

In addition to these projects, teachers might use PowerPoint construction on any topic as an excellent project to assess at-risk students' learning.

Summary

At-risk students require teachers to use special strategies so that they can truly determine what students know and can do before instruction, during instruction, and after it. Teachers could begin by assessing students' social skills and understanding the kinds of assessment that works best with them. The teacher should plan preassessments, informal assessments, formative and summative that capture students' content knowledge and affective experiences.

4

English and Social Studies Assessments with Moderate to No Scaffolding

Planning assessments for the "regular" or "average" student should be the easiest to do because most resources address the needs of these kinds of students. However, we realize that within this group called "average," we have differing academic strengths, interests, and learning styles; therefore, it is important for the teacher to find out as much as possible about these students keeping in mind cognitive stages of development and psychosocial issues. Even within the realm of the "average" student, we can find great variety in a "regular" (i.e., not special education or gifted) classroom.

This chapter shows teachers specific examples of differentiated assessment strategies leveled for students who have average readiness needs. After providing an overview of these students, it provides examples of preassesssments, formative assessments, and summative assessments. For formative assessments it provides information about using the Differentiating Assessment: Six-Part Template. What follows is a brief summary of developmental issues that can have an impact on how we differentiate assessment for "regular" or "average" students, Part 1 of the six-part assessment process.

Students' Needs—Who Are the Average Students?

Cognitive Development

From ages 6 or 7 years all the way up to 11 or 12 years, which can include some sixth- and seventh-grade students, children are *just beginning* to think logically; they are still in what Piaget calls the "concrete operational stage" of cognitive development (Ginn,

2003). They can reverse a process and see different perspectives; however, they continue to see the future as an extension of the present, and they are still quite concrete. They have not begun to think abstractly. As teachers think about the assessment tasks they plan for 11 or 12 year olds, they may need to remember that some of them could still be functioning at this level, and this is *normal*. I am highlighting normal because many teachers may consider those students who are still in the concrete operational stage as delayed, and they may feel a need to refer those students to a remedial or learning disabled program. This practice denies the reality of normal development.

If a student is still at the concrete operational stage, teachers cannot expect him or her to predict or infer as well as those students who have moved into a higher stage of cognitive development. Because these students continue to see the future as an extension of the present, they may not be able to abstract a future event or draw a conclusion based on reading between the lines in a text, especially about topics that are foreign to them. These students could also have trouble understanding abstract or even some concrete concepts. Teachers who teach conceptually need to realize that some students may not be able to understand those concepts until they are older. Some theorists, for example, Hilda Taba (1971) disagree with Piaget's stages. She believes that teachers can move students beyond the confines of a concrete operational stage by conducting a "concept development" process. I have used this process and agree with her to some extent; however, I can still see that some of our average students struggle to think conceptually and inferentially.

From ages 11 or 12 years to adulthood, students can be expected to begin joining the "formal operations stage" of cognitive development. When students are just entering this stage, they may be highly critical because they are still idealistic. This idealism and the tendency to argue with reality characterize many middle school students. Knowing this tendency helps teachers plan assessments that capitalize on this stage of development. Another aspect of this stage that helps teachers with assessment is realizing that some of the younger students (11 or 12 years) may not be able to adequately use metacognitive skills. Research has supported the benefits of teachers encouraging students to use metacognitive skills to help them learn more efficiently; however, if a student has not developed that capacity, the teacher could set him or her up for frustration if appropriate scaffolding is not provided until the student is competent.

As teachers think about "normal" or "average" students, especially those who are 11 or 12 year olds, they need to remember that some of them may struggle with abstract thinking, which includes problems with metacognitive processing, inferring, and thinking conceptually. Teachers need to be prepared to scaffold assessments for these students.

Psychosocial Development

When teachers plan assessments that address the learning needs of the "average" student, they need to understand some of the psychosocial issues with which they are dealing. Teachers need to realize that their students are in the process of developing a sense of identity and that how teachers assess them and give them feedback about their competence or lack of it can help shape that identity (Erikson, 1950). *Attributional theory* (Weiner, 1985) reminds teachers that some students internalize achievement, and others externalize it. If teachers want to be a positive influence in how our 11- to 18-year-old students develop their identities, they need to pay attention to how students view themselves in their abilities to succeed in teachers' assessment of their work. Teachers need to realize the impact they have on the developing identity and be gentle, but fair and firm with their assessments. Assessment procedures could damage students' developing identities if teachers do not approach them appropriately.

Gradual Release of Scaffolding

As you will see with some of the examples of assessments that are useful in the regular classroom, it is important to use scaffolding no longer than it is necessary to support students' development of a skill or concept. Teachers must have a clear idea of students' readiness to perform independently. This sensitivity to students' needs is critical as teachers design summative assessments. If they take away the scaffolding prematurely or assess learning too soon, students may be frustrated and feel and sense of failure. The best way to determine when to ask students to do something independently is when they are sustaining an 80 percent mastery or better on formative assessments. Teachers will know if they have released scaffolding too soon if numbers of students do not succeed on summative assessments.

Using the Textbook to Design Units with Moderate to No Scaffolding

Many teachers rely heavily on the textbook to provide assessments of learning. This can be a problem if the textbook is not an appropriate resource for all of the essential knowledge and skills teachers plan to teach based on the standards of their curriculum. Often teachers ask students to read a chapter in the textbook and then answer the questions at the end of that chapter. Most students devote little or no attention to how they are answering those questions. They simply find the answers in the textbook, write them down, and then forget about them. If teachers want to use the textbook as a resource in the regular classroom, they might get ideas for questions from it, but they should go well beyond those textbook ideas to make the assessment meaningful for students. If teachers do not take the step of putting the textbook assessment into their own words and aligning those assessments with their own planned unit, the students will waste valuable time.

English/Language Arts Examples of Preassessments: Determining Readiness, Learning Styles, and Interests

If teachers are planning a unit of study for a regular English/language arts class, they may want to, as soon as possible, assess students' reading abilities, learning styles, and interests because regular students have vast differences, and the teacher needs to be prepared to respond to those differences (see Northey, 2005 and Waterman, 2007 for a full range of preassessment tools). Teachers also need to continue to preassess students for each new unit of study because research has told us that students' learning styles are not stable, their interests are subject to shifting, and even their reading abilities can vary depending on the content.

Procedures

One of the most important things a language arts teacher might want to preassess is student attitude toward reading and books. See Figure 3.5 (p. 62) for a "Reading Survey" to give regular students.

To Scaffold

Regular students should be able to complete this survey with the examples provided in writing. They could write and then share their answers question by question as a whole class or the teacher could allow them to discuss the survey in small groups. See Figure 3.6 (p. 63) for an "Important Book and Literary History Assessment."

Teachers should assign this survey for regular students and expect them to be able to make unassisted presentations to the class. They might give extra credit to those who bring in the book or make a poster about it. They could also require students to write about their book using a prompt such as this: "Write a letter to a friend or family member recommending your important book. Remember to use the correct format for a friendly letter and to use appropriate language, organization, style, and standard English conventions."

English/Language Arts and Social Studies Examples of Preassessments: Content

Anticipation Guide

Figure 4.1 is social studies example of an Anticipation Guide (Herber, 1978) for regular students. Each statement follows the sequence of the text. The vocabulary is slightly more difficult than that used for at-risk students, and the statements require students to infer. The way to conduct a lesson using this Anticipation Guide is as follows:

Procedures

Step 1: Hand out the Anticipation Guide as students enter the room.

Step 2: Ask students to either read the statements to themselves or, depending on the level of the class, ask volunteers or use demand response to have students read each statement out loud. Ask the class to decide if they agree (A) or disagree (D) with the statement. Ask students to read the statements aloud, then ask them to raise their hands to indicate agreement or disagreement for each statement. Assure students that if they are wrong, then they could actually learn more than if they guess correctly.

Step 3: Monitor students as they put A's or D's in the correct boxes.

Step 4: After going through the statements and having students indicate agreement or disagreement, decide how to read the chapters in the book. Depending on the capabilities of the class, have students take turns reading to find the answers; use pairs reading to each other, groups reading to each other, or individuals reading silently.

Step 5: Next, ask students to read the statement on the Anticipation Guide and then to read the statement in the textbook that proves the statement true or false.

If teachers have students read to themselves, it is a good idea to add a fourth column (a suggestion by social studies teacher Don Dixon). Figure 4.1 includes that fourth column, which is an adjustment to the traditional Anticipation Guide.

Figure 4.1. Anticipation Guide

Read the statements below and decide if you AGREE (A) or DISAGREE (D) with each statement. Write your answer in the left column under Anticipate. After you have learned about the topic from your textbook, complete the right column under React. Notice what you have learned.

Anticipate	Statement	React	Paragraph Number and Page Number
	1. After the War of 1812, it became apparent that North Carolina had changed in three major ways.		
	2. The two main causes of North Carolina's problems were the war and slavery.		
	3. North Carolina had no public schools in the early 1800s; instead there were academies.		
	4. Eli Whitney's invention of the cotton gin in 1793 affected the state's economy.		
	5. In 1819, the U.S. government made all the Native Americans living in North Carolina leave their land.		
	6. The North Carolina government was democratic in form and spirit although there were problems.		
	7. The North Carolina legislature set up a literary fund that published Archibald Murphy's book on education reform.		
	8. The internal improvements funded by the General Assembly were highly successful in improving the North Carolina economy.		
	9. North Carolina had an undemocratic constitution that needed to be reformed.		
	10. Archibald Murphy was a social activist.		

Key: 1. D; 2. D; 3. A; 4. A; 5. D; 6. A ; 7. D; 8. D ; 9. A; 10. A

3-2-1 Adaptation for Average Students: English Example—Science Fiction

If teachers are beginning a unit on any English or social studies topic with average students, they should take into consideration that they should have *some* prior knowledge that is directly or indirectly associated with the unit of study. Figure 4.2 is a 3-2-1 example that will help teachers assess students' prior knowledge.

Figure 4.2. 3-2-1 Process and Procedures

Average students may need an example to get them started, but they should be able to write at least three things they know about most English or social studies topics. For example, if the teacher asks students to list three things they know about "science fiction," they should be able to recall reading works of science fiction in elementary school. For social studies, average students may not recall details about the civil war, but they should be able to think of examples of the effects of war in their daily lives. They should be able to write two questions and one way they would like to learn about the topic. By asking average students their questions and how they want to learn about a topic, the teacher will be better able to tailor the instruction to meet their needs.

This 3-2-1 assessment is a short and easy way to preassess average students' knowledge, questions, and learning styles regarding a topic in English/language arts or social studies. Teachers can easily use it as a "ticket out the door" assignment. Teachers could hand out cards that look like Figure 4.3.

Figure 4.3. 3-2-1 Assessment of Science Fiction

3-2-1

1. Write **3** things you already know about science fiction.

2. Write **2** questions you have about science fiction.

3. Write **1** way you would like to learn about this topic.

Informal Assessments

Vocabulary Ball Game—Social Studies

Most average students should be able to handle informal assessments that include playing a game with a ball. Figure 4.4 is an example of an assessment using a ball as a prop.

Figure 4.4. Vocabulary Ball Game: Social Studies

Procedures

Step 1: Ask students to review the unit on "Reconstruction" to identify and define the key terms listed there. Ask them to make flash cards with the term on the front and the definition on the back.

Step 2: Allow time for partners to practice learning the definitions of the terms.

Step 3: Show students how to play a ball game with the social studies terms. The game goes like this. Throw the ball to a student who catches it. When the student catches the ball, either give him or her a term to define or give him or her the definition and the student supplies the term.

Step 4: If the student correctly identifies the term or gives the correct definition, then he or she throws the ball to someone else. When that student catches the ball, the student who threw it either gives a term or the definition of a term, and the student who caught the ball must give the correct answer. If the student misses the term, he or she must throw the ball back to the teacher instead of to a classmate.

Another way to do this is to have the teacher ask all the questions and students throw the ball to each other.

Formative Assessments

Formative assessments allow teachers to determine if their students are learning what the teacher is teaching them. What follows are several examples of differentiated formative assessment strategies that will help the teacher scaffold assessment for average students. For each assessment example, teachers will see examples of how to address Parts 2 through 5. The first part of the chapter covered Part 1 for all examples, and teachers can only complete Part 6 after they have implemented the assessment. Figure 4.5 is a review of the template for this process.

Figure 4.5. Differentiating Assessment: Six-Part Template

1. Students' Needs (described in detail)				
2. Curriculum				
Standard Course of Study (SCOS)	Essential Question (EQ)	Know	Understand	Do *(See MO below)*
3. Measurable Objective (MO)				
Introduction	Thinking Verb(s)	Product	Response Criterion	Content
4. Differentiation				
Readiness		Interests		Learning Styles
5. Assessment Procedures (listed by steps)				
6. Assessment Audit				

Differentiated Formative Assessments by Learning Styles

For the assessment strategies that follow, I will show how to plan differentiated and strategic assessments for average students. I will explain how to use categorizations discussed in Silver, Strong, and Perini (2007): mastery, understanding, self-expression, interpersonal, and four-style. I have adapted (including using alternative names for some similar concepts) their descriptions of these best practices, and I have focused on their usefulness as English and social studies assessment strategies for average students.

Mastery-Based Assessments: Graduated Difficulty

Document-Based Questions

This is a perfect strategy to use to assess average students' English and social studies learning. It is adapted from Mosston (1977) and Silver, Strong, and Perini (2007). Teachers begin with easy processes and increase the difficulty as students demonstrate skills through formative assessments. For average students, teachers should expect that they will be able to eventually master the material in their textbook. They may not be able to master material that gifted or highly advanced students can master, but they should be able to master grade level material. If teachers graduate difficulty for average students, they may not need too much scaffolding. Figure 4.6 is an integrated English-social studies example about answering document-based questions (DBQs).

Figure 4.6. Document-Based Questions

Curriculum				
SCOS	**EQ:** How do primary documents help us answer important social questions?	**Know**—how to use primary sources to answer important questions, how to write answers clearly, sufficiently, and accurately.	**Understand** that using primary sources helps us answer important social questions.	**Do**—use primary sources to answer important social questions (*see MO below*).

Measurable Objective				
Introduction	**Thinking Verb(s)**	**Product**	**Response Criterion**	**Content**
Students will...	classify, organize, execute, interpret, and produce	written answers to document-based questions	that are thorough and accurate	based on primary sources related to a social studies topic.

Differentiation		
Readiness—gradual release of responsibility with graduated difficulty scaffolds assessment	**Interests**—allowing students to choose sources of information increases their level of interest	**Style**—mastery, analytical, linguistic, investigative

Procedures

Step 1: Activate learning by starting with a question average students will be able to answer. For example, "What is a primary source of information?" Use "think-pair-share" or "think-write-pair-share," and then ask students to share with the whole class. This process allows the teacher to assess students' prior knowledge and interest in this topic.

Step 2: Present basic information about primary sources in real-world (nontextbook) terms. For example introduce the concept that primary sources include diaries, journals, political documents, cartoons, and interviews. Provide several examples of primary sources for students to examine. When students seem to understand primary sources, ask them to go online or examine hard copies of information to find examples of their own. The class could talk about the kinds of questions primary sources might answer.

Assessment 1

Step 3: To determine if students understand the concept of document-based questions (DBQs), ask them to write at least five questions based on the primary sources they found. Having them write questions based on primary sources of interest to them will help them better understand how to answer questions based on primary sources with which they are less familiar. Students should find this assessment enjoyable and interesting.

Step 4: After students have completed Assessment 1, increase the difficulty to include instructing them about writing complete answers to document–based questions. Make sure students understand how to turn a question into a statement or claim. Explain to them how to support that statement or claim with examples that they paraphrase or quote from the primary source or sources. Model this process and ask students to practice until all of them seem to understand how to answer DBQs.

Assessment 2

Step 5: Assign students to answer their own DBQs using the speaker, occasion, audience, purpose, subject (SOAPS) graphic organizers to plan their response. Evaluate what students write in the graphic organizer and offer helpful feedback so that when they write their responses, they may have a better chance of writing sufficiently and accurately. Figure 4.7 is the SOAPS graphic organizer.

Figure 4.7. SOAPS Graphic Organizer

Category	Information Gathered from Primary Document
Speaker	
Occasion	
Audience	
Purpose	
Subject	

From http://www.edmond.k12.OK.US/socialstudies/SOAPS%20Intro.pdf

Assessment 3

Step 6: After students have received feedback on their response plans, ask them to fully answer at least two of the DBQs they wrote. Next, ask them to find a partner for peer editing. After peers have helped students determine if they have answered the questions appropriately, evaluate their answers.

Assessment 4 and On

Step 6: Give students increasingly difficult DBQs that you or students construct and that are related to units of study, or use DBQs from sources such as AP guides or from the large number of resources online.

Teams-Games-Tournaments

Figure 4.8 is an English or social studies example of this popular strategy that should work well with average students. It is adapted from the work of DeVries, Edwards, and Salvin (1978) and Silver, Strong, and Perini (2007).

Figure 4.8. Teams-Games-Tournament for English and Social Studies

Curriculum				
SCOS	**EQ:** What are important facts to remember for an English or social studies topic?	**Know**—vocabulary terms for a specific English or social studies topic.	**Understand** that practice and teamwork help us better remember important facts for English or social studies topics.	**Do**— participate in a tournament to learn facts about an English or social studies topic (*see MO below*).

Measurable Objective				
Introduction	**Thinking Verb(s)**	**Product**	**Response Criterion**	**Content**
Students will…	recall	short answers	that are correct	important English or social studies facts.

Differentiation		
Readiness—teacher-guided process scaffolds assessment	**Interests**—can allow students to choose the terms for review to increase interest in content; earning points for a team also increases interest in achieving	**Style**—interpersonal, mastery, visual, kinesthetic (pulling cards)

Procedures

Take the following steps to set it up.

Step 1: Divide the class into groups. Each group should have one relatively high-functioning student who is labeled "advanced," two or more middle-functioning students who are labeled "average," and one low-functioning student who is labeled "novice" or other innocuous designation. Limit the teams to four students to make the competition flow more easily.

Step 2: Make a set of review cards for each table. An adaptation could be to ask students to make the questions with the following directions: For English and social studies the questions should include vocabulary or questions that have only one right answer. Number the cards to correspond with the answer key.

Step 3: Appoint a group leader (the highest functioning student), who will help the students take turns and will check answers. Students practice answering the questions on the cards to prepare for the tournament.

Step 4: The tournament can be the same day as the practice or the next day depending on the amount of class time available. Make sure each table has a set of cards and a key. All questions and keys should be the same; however, the teacher may color code the cards to designate teams. The teams could choose their color in advance. They could also have a team name.

Step 5: When it is time for the tournament to begin, give the signal that the students designated "advanced" should go to the "advanced" table. Students designated "average" can go to the two "average tables." The students designated "novice" should go to the "novice table."

Step 6: The students proceed with the game as follows: Students take turns pulling a card from the stack of cards. The appointed or elected leader of the group checks to see that the student has answered the question correctly. This leadership role might rotate depending how often students play the game. Students earn points for their home group.

Step 7: After each table has gone through all the cards or if time has run out, players return to their home teams to record and tally their total points. The winning team gets an A, the second-place a B, and the other teams get a C. No one fails. Take a running total of team points to conduct a celebration at the end of the year and a special acknowledgment for winning teams.

Students enjoy this process, and the teacher gets a good idea of how much students are learning.

Understanding-Based Formative or Summative Assessments

Concept Attainment

This strategy (Figure 4.9) includes assessing students' abilities to explore in depth what complex words might mean.

Figure 4.9. Concept Attainment

Curriculum				
SCOS	**EQ:** How do we evaluate conflict in a literary work?	**Know**—the types of conflict and how we define those types.	**Understand** that conflict occurs in a literary work when a human or humans go against themselves or against an archetype or archetypal forces.	**Do**—use the process of concept development to learn about conflict in all literary work *(see MO below)*.

Measurable Objective				
Introduction	**Thinking Verb(s)**	**Product**	**Response Criterion**	**Content**
Students will…	generate, classify, compare, and organize	an organized list	that defines in detail	the types of conflict.

Differentiation		
Readiness— a teacher-led process scaffolds assessment	**Interests**—suspense and guessing create interest	**Style**—understanding, visual, investigative

Procedures

Average students might learn a great deal about complex concepts using Jerome Bruner's process of concept attainment outlined below, which is adapted from http://www.csus.edu/indiv/p/pfeiferj/EdTe226/concept%20attainment/ca_form.doc (accessed October 11, 2008); and from Bruner (1973).

Bruner's Concept Attainment—English Example

Step 1: Select an English concept, such as "conflict in a literary work." Next determine attributes that would fit under the "no" and the "yes" column. Make cards that are large enough for the student to see the attributes listed on each card. Cards for this example would look like the box below and have double-face tape on the backs so that you can attach them to the chart.

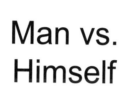

Positive examples are man versus man, man versus nature, man versus animal, man versus society.

Negative examples are yes versus no, the world versus the universe, reasonable versus unreasonable, time versus money, gold versus silver.

Step 2: Hand out the following worksheet so that students might record what is happening on the board.

Student Worksheet

Concept Attainment

Student name:_____

Yes	No

Step 3: Show the cards one at a time to the students. For the first card, "man versus himself," say, "This card is a 'yes.'" For the next card, which could be "yes versus no," say, "This card is a 'no.'" Repeat this process until there are three examples on the board.

Step 4: Ask students to look at the "Yes" column and ask what the yes answers have in common. Tell students not to say out loud what they notice.

Step 5: Hold up the next three cards and ask students to say in which column they should go. Some students will get it and others may not. Ask students to offer more examples, and prompt them to reveal the concept, which is "conflict occurs in a literary work when a human or humans go against themselves or against an archetype or archetypal forces."

Step 6: Facilitate a discussion among students so that they might evaluate the process and talk about how they might apply it to future concept-attainment activities.

Real-World Problem Solving

This strategy is an excellent way to formatively assess average students' learning because it shows how an academic topic applies to the real world. Figure 4.10 (p. 117) is a social studies example of this strategy.

Procedures

Average students would enjoy a chance to participate in a real-world problem-solving assessment process, but teachers must not make it too open-ended. Therefore, they could offer problem choices and give students specific guidelines for solving it. Figure 4.11 (p. 118) is an example of a syllabus teachers might use to solve a real world social studies problem.

Figure 4.10. Real-World Problem Solving

Curriculum				
SCOS	**EQ:** What is the best process for solving a real-world social studies problem?	**Know**—how to research a social studies topic to solve a real problem; how to construct a product (such as a brochure, PowerPoint presentation, or booklet) to show how to solve the problem; and how to find more information about the topic related to the problem.	**Understand** that research can help us find information to help solve important problems in the real world.	**Do**—use research to offer solutions to a real social studies problem *(see MO below)*.

Measurable Objective				
Introduction	**Thinking Verb(s)**	**Product**	**Response Criterion**	**Content**
Students will...	generate, plan, produce, create, implement, organize, and evaluate	a solution to a real-world problem	that is an efficient, effective, and creative	solution to a real-world social studies problem.

Differentiation		
Readiness—checkpoints to assure students are proceeding as they should; scaffold assessment	**Interests**—students choose from a list of projects	**Style**—understanding, creative, investigative

Figure 4.11. Syllabus for Real-World Social Studies Problem

Syllabus for Solving a Real-World Social
Studies Problem: Southern Africa

Step 1: Choose a problem from the ones listed below related to the unit on "Southern Africa."

 ◆ Problem 1: In the Sahel, south of the Sahara desert, drought is causing a process called desertification. Find out what is causing desertification and what you might do to address the problem. Make a brochure, PowerPoint presentation, or booklet that might help us to better understand the problem.

 ◆ Problem 2: The process of colonization by European cultures created conflicts among ethnic groups. What are the conflicts and how are they affecting the current southern African society today? Make a brochure, PowerPoint presentation, or booklet that you might show to a group of students and their parents about ethnic conflict in southern Africa or in a specific country in that region.

 ◆ Problem 3: Although the slave trade ended many years ago, the people of southern Africa can still feel its effects. What did the slave trade do to the families and villages in southern Africa? Design a brochure, PowerPoint presentation, or booklet to explain the effects of slavery on southern African culture and what is its effect today in Africa and in the United States?

Step 2: Find at least three sources of information to inform your work. Make sure to cite these sources in MLA form.

Step 3: What follows are the dates parts of the project are due:

 ◆ Your decision about the problem you will address and where you plan to find information:

 Date due: _____

 ◆ Notes you have taken on the topic.

 Date due:_____

 ◆ Plan for the product

 Date due:_____

 ◆ Product

 Date due:_____

Use the following rubric (Figure 4.12) to make sure you are on the right track.

Figure 4.12. Rubric for Real-World Problem

Criteria	Level 1	Level 2	Level 3	Level 4
Content	The amount of information included in the product does not sufficiently cover the topic and/or many of the facts are inaccurate.	The amount of information included in the product leaves out many important ideas and/or includes some ideas that are inaccurate.	The product includes enough ideas to adequately cover the topic and all ideas are accurate.	The product includes in-depth and accurate information that exceeds the expectations for the product.
Organization	The information in the product appears to be arranged in a random manner.	The information in the product is arranged so that it is hard to follow and confusing.	The information in the product is well organized and easy to follow.	The organization of the product matches exceptionally well with the information.
Style	The writing style is simple, has many grammatical errors, and is sloppy.	The writing style is uninteresting and often distracts from the ideas generated as the solution.	The writing style is adequate and expresses the ideas generated as the solution in a clear and concise manner.	The writing style creates interest and enthusiasm for the solution. The writing includes excellent use of literary devices.
Originality	The information is taken directly from a source with no attempt to synthesize it.	The information is not presented in a way that differs much from the sources from which it was taken.	The product is creative and interesting and shows a synthesis of the information.	The product is very interesting and shows an exceptionally creative solution to the problem.

Note that for average students, the problem assessment should not be too open-ended, teachers should require checkpoints to make sure students are proceeding as they should, and the rubric is written in terms that students should be able to understand (the teacher should make sure students understand it by asking them to paraphrase it either orally or in writing).

Self-Expression-Based Formative Assessments

Pattern Maker

This strategy (Figure 4.13) is a great tool for assessing students' English or social studies leaning. Also known as extrapolation, it is a way to help average students see how noting patterns can help them create or problem solve. It was adapted from the work of Gick and Holyoak (1980) and Silver, Strong, and Perini (2007).

Figure 4.13. Pattern Maker

Curriculum				
SCOS	**EQ:** How can we use a pattern from one thing to help us create or discover the same patterns in other things?	**Know**—how to use an analogue of an eyewitness account as a model from which to write another eyewitness account.	**Understand** that looking at patterns in an analogue can help us create or discover those same patterns in similar things.	**Do**—use an analogue (an eyewitness account) to write another eyewitness account (*see MO below*).

Measurable Objective				
Introduction	**Thinking Verb(s)**	**Product**	**Response Criterion**	**Content**
Students will…	generate, compare, organize, note, and	record patterns in an analogous eyewitness account to write an eyewitness account	that is sufficient, accurate, organized, and interesting	about an incident students choose to record and share with others.

Differentiation		
Readiness—teacher modeling scaffolds assessment	**Interests**—students allowed to choose their topic for an eyewitness account	**Style**—self-expression, investigative, analytical, visual

Eyewitness Account: Procedures

In this assessment, teachers provide one or more "analogues" which are the sources of the pattern or patterns. For average students they must help students see patterns of the analogue as they apply to new problems. Assessment includes determining how well the students accurately identify the structure of the analogue and how they apply that understanding to solve a problem or create a product.

Step 1: Ask students to read an eyewitness account of an historical event.

Step 2: Ask students to note any patterns they see. They might note organization, transitions, 5 W's (details), sequencing, perspective, plot line, and so forth.

Step 3: Direct students to record patterns they see using a graphic organizer that you have filled in for them or that is blank so that students might supply the categories and information. Figure 4.14 is a graphic organizer to help students record patterns in an analogous eyewitness account.

Figure 4.14. Graphic Organizer of Patterns

Patterns in Eyewitness Accounts

Categories	Information
Organization pattern	
Content: who, what, when, where, why, and how	
Point of view	
Sequencing	
Plot line: basic situation, rising action, climax, resolution	

Step 4: Ask students to think about how they used the analogues presented to help them see the patterns that they might use to write their own eyewitness account.

Step 5: Students write their own eyewitness accounts of any topic they choose. Peers should edit the first draft or drafts, and then the teacher should evaluate it.

Step 6: Give feedback to help students revise until the account is at standard or above.

Visualizing

The following strategy (Figure 4.15) can assess students' abilities to translate written or spoken words into pictures. Average students should already have some experience with this process but might need some encouragement and review to put visualization into practice. It should help average students better visualize, remember, and understand important concepts and skills.

Figure 4.15. Social Studies Example of Visualization: "The Progressive Era"

Curriculum				
SCOS	**EQ:** How can we use visualizing to help us understand the Progressive Era (1890–1920)?	**Know**—how to use visualizing to understand an historical era, how to put words into pictures.	**Understand** that using visualization helps us to better understand the Progressive Era (1890–1920).	**Do**—visualize written words and convert them into drawings *(see MO below)*.

Measurable Objective				
Introduction	Thinking Verb(s)	Product	Response Criterion	Content
Students will…	exemplify and create	pictures	accurately depicting	problems of the Progressive Era.

Differentiation		
Readiness—teacher-guided process scaffolds assessment; teacher checks constantly for understanding while circulating around the room	**Interests**—students allowed to use creativity in their drawings	**Style**—self-expression, visual, creative, verbal/linguistic

Procedures

Step 1: Explain to students that you will be assessing their ability to visualize and record that visualization on a piece of paper. Hand each student an 8×10-inch piece of white paper and make sure all students have pencils and possibly some means of coloring what they draw.

Step 2: Tell students that they will be using a visualizing method to help them learn about challenging problems that existed during the Progressive Era. Tell them that as you read, you want them to draw what they hear. Next tell them that they must first prepare the space for their drawing. Tell them to divide the paper into four boxes. Model each of these steps and show students what the paper should look like. Next ask them to title the picture "Progressive Era Problems" and ask them to put their name beside the title (Figure 4.16).

Figure 4.16. Four-Box for Visualizing

Progressive Era by_____(student's name)

Step 3: Next tell students they are going to practice the process of visualizing and then drawing.

Step 4: Tell students you are going to read them a description of a major problem that existed during the Progressive Era. Tell them that drawing what they hear will help them to better understand this era in American history.

Step 5: Read descriptions of problems such as: homelessness, poverty, child labor, and poor sanitation. Ask students to draw what they hear. They should draw a different problem in each of the boxes they have created by folding their paper.

Step 6: After students have completed the drawings, collect and evaluate the work. Ask student volunteers to share their work.

Teachers can choose to give students a summative assessment to determine if they have developed a deeper understanding of the specific problems from the Progressive Era. They can also evaluate if students use this process on their own to better understand aspects of history.

Interpersonal-Based Assessments

Interpersonal-based assessments use students' natural inclination to help each other as they work together. These kinds of assessments should motivate average students especially if the teacher offers the right amount of structuring and enthusiasm.

Jigsaw

This cooperative learning assessment (Figure 4.17) works well with average students. It was adapted from Aronson et al. (1978).

Figure 4.17. Jigsaw Types of Poetry

Curriculum				
SCOS	EQ: How do people use various types of poetry to express themselves?	Know—how to teach others about various poetry, information about various types of poems, how to work effectively in a group.	Understand that people use various types of poetry to express their feelings, ideas, and stories.	Do—read about different types of poetry, plan how to teach the information to peers, teach the information, and assess the learning (see MO below).

Measurable Objective				
Introduction	Thinking Verb(s)	Product	Response Criterion	Content
Students will…	summarize, compare, explain, organize, differentiate, plan, and produce	teaching materials	that adequately and accurately	explore types of poems.

Differentiation		
Readiness—teacher-guided process scaffolds assessment	Interests—working in a group to learn together, choosing how to teach a topic	Style—interpersonal, investigative, visual and auditory, verbal/linguistic

Procedures: Jigsaw—Types of Poetry

Here is an example of using Jigsaw as a way to assess students' learning an English topic. Teachers should use this activity as they explore types of poetry such as the following: lyric poetry, free verse, ballad, and sonnet.

Step 1: Put each student in a home group and ask them to number off one through four. If there are an uneven number of students, make a group of five. There may be several groups of four or five.

Step 2: Assign students who are number 4 (and 5) to read about lyric poems and one or more examples of them, students who are number 3 to read about free verse poems and one or more examples of them, students who are number 2 to read about ballads and one or more examples of them, and assign students who are number 1 to read about sonnets and one or more examples of them.

Step 3: Instruct students to move to a 1 table, a 2 table, a 3 table, and a 4 table. Tell students at each table that they should read their assignment and complete some products with which to teach their home group about their topic. Structure this activity by giving students blank white paper or poster paper, cards, and markers so that they might construct some flashcards or posters that teach about their topic. Ask students to make a five-problem quiz to test their home group members' knowledge of their topic. Students should make a quiz for each member of their home group. The groups should have four or five members.

Step 4: When students return to their home groups, they should take turns teaching that group about their type of poem. They should administer their assessment and turn it in to the teacher after they evaluate it.

Community Circle

Figure 4.18 shows a way to allow students a chance to voice their thoughts, feelings, and values. It was adapted from Silver, Strong, and Perini (2007). It is not to be confused with a Socratic seminar, which assesses what students might have learned about a topic.

Procedures

This process is more like a classroom meeting during which the teacher might assess concerns students are having about an issue in class, or the teacher could use it to assess students' prior knowledge and understanding of an English or social studies topic. The process works best for most students if they are in a circle.

The following are some possible English and social studies topics that average student might enjoy discussing:

- ◆ English
  - Why is it important to be able to express yourself in writing?
  - How is English useful when we study other subjects such as social studies, science, or geography?
  - Why is it important to be able to closely analyze literature?
  - Why is it important to use conventions of grammar and spelling when we write?
  - What are the most important uses of writing?
  - Why should everyone learn to analyze a story or novel?

Figure 4.18. Community Circle

Curriculum				
SCOS	**EQ:** What are our thoughts and feelings about important topics in English and social studies?	**Know**—how to share ideas with others without monopolizing.	**Understand** that discussing thoughts and feelings can change our perspective or deepen our knowledge of important topics in English and social studies.	**Do**—participate in a discussion of an important English or social studies topic, share ideas and feelings *(see MO below).*

Measurable Objective				
Introduction	**Thinking Verb(s)**	**Product**	**Response Criterion**	**Content**
Students will…	explain, summarize, and produce	oral responses	that are on topic, honest, and complete	about a variety of English or social studies topics.

Differentiation		
Readiness—teacher-guided process scaffolds assessment	**Interests**—group discussion is motivating; students enjoy sharing their opinions and ideas	**Style**—interpersonal, verbal/linguistic, auditory

- ◆ Social Studies
  - Why is it important to learn to see patterns in history?
  - Why is it critical to learn the five themes of geography?
  - What does it mean to think like a social scientist?
  - How might the ability to analyze social problems have an impact on the well-being of our contemporary culture?
  - Why is technology important to social studies?
  - Why do we study history?
  - How do humans affect the quality of a government?
  - Why is it important to learn about the economy of different cultures?
  - How does geography affect where people live and what they do?

- What invention most changed our world?
- Why do we need maps and other technologies to understand our world?
- Why is it important to learn about the Depression?

Four-Style Assessment

Window Notes

Figure 4. 19 shows a way of assessing several aspects of what students are gaining from a lesson. It was adapted from Silver, Strong, Perini, and Tuculescu (2003) and Silver, Strong, and Perini (2007).

Figure 4.19. Window Notes

Curriculum				
SCOS	**EQ:** What was the Great Depression?	**Know**—how to make notes in four ways to understand the Great Depression.	**Understand** that the Great Depression changed the way people view economic health.	**Do**— make notes based on facts, feelings, questions, and ideas about the Great Depression *(see MO below)*.

Measurable Objective				
Introduction	**Thinking Verb(s)**	**Product**	**Response Criterion**	**Content**
Students will…	summarize, produce, exemplify, attribute, generate, and implement	window notes	that accurately and thoroughly note facts, feelings, questions, and ideas	about the Great Depression.

Differentiation		
Readiness—teacher-guided process and graphic organizer scaffolds assessment	**Interests**—students choose the four aspects of the notes to take	**Style**—interpersonal, understanding, mastery, and self-expression

Procedures

For window notes teachers might assess the following: the facts students are recording, how they feel about that information, what questions they have about it, and what ideas they have about how they might use that topic. What follows are general steps and then an example for a social studies topic.

Step 1: Announce to students that they will be taking notes about the lesson in a new way.

Step 2: Hand out an 8×10 piece of white paper and model how to divide into 4 equal boxes.

Step 3: Ask students to label each of the boxes as follows:

- Facts

- Feelings

- Questions

- Ideas

Step 4: As you talk about the topic, ask students to write in the boxes they have created. Steps 4 and 5 show a social studies example of taking notes on the Great Depression.

Step 4: *(For Social Studies)* Assuming the you have completed steps 1–3, the next step is to explain that the class will be learning about the Great Depression. For average students, you might want them to listen to a song such as "Brother Can You Spare a Dime?," and you might ask them to infer what the Great Depression might be about from that song and from their prior knowledge of the word depression.

Step 5: Instruct the students to read about the Great Depression in their textbooks or another text. Instruct them to collect facts, feelings, questions, and ideas in the correct boxes as they come to them. For this Window Note, students should find at least 7 facts, 7 feelings, 7 questions, and 7 ideas. Allow students to share one at a time from each of the 4 boxes. Collect this work and evaluate it, but then return it to students so that they can keep it in a notebook for studying purposes. (The number 7 is adjustable.)

Note: With all of these assessments, it is important to rotate them so that students have an opportunity to experience each type of assessment.

Summative Assessments for Average Students

Constructing Summative Assessments for Average Students

Teachers can use textbook-generated true/false, short-answer, matching, and multiple choice tests because the textbook levels them for average students. However, teachers should evaluate these textbook resources based on the criteria listed in Chapter 2 and keep in mind that these tests might not always fit the needs of the class; therefore, they might need to construct their own tests. Keeping in mind that these types of tests, especially multiple choice, align with high-stakes testing, makes familiarizing students with their "grammar" important. Until, or if, the present culture of accountability through multiple-choice, norm-based standardized testing, ceases to be, students should have practice throughout the year to demonstrate what they know through multiple-choice assessments. Teachers need to make sure their multiple-choice classroom assessments align with the high-stakes tests.

Crossword Puzzles as Summative Assessments

To use crossword puzzles or other word puzzles as a summative assessment for regular students, the teacher may or may not choose to provide a word list. Average students should be able to solve a crossword puzzle as a test without teacher help. Having a puzzle to solve rather than a test to take can make this assessment more interesting and less stressful for students. The teacher can assign a regular student or students who are interested in technology and interested in the unit to create a crossword puzzle for the class as an independent differentiated assignment.

Extended-Writing Response

Figure 4.20 offers some essay prompts for English and social studies. Notice that the prompts are somewhat longer for average students than for at-risk students.

Figure 4.20. Writing Prompts

English Writing Prompts for Average Students

1. The educational leaders who oversee the curriculum for elementary through high school require that all students study literature. Explain why you think these leaders made that decision and how their decision affects you.
2. Think of a novel you have read that has an important theme. Explain how the author used various literary techniques to develop that theme for the audience.
3. Choose a work of art and a poem that have similar themes or topics. Explain how these two works are similar and how they are different.

4. Think of an important event in your life and describe it clearly so your audience can clearly understand what happened and what it meant to you.

Social Studies Writing Prompts for Average Students

1. Take a side in a controversial topic, such as abortion, gun control, or the Iraq war, and convince your audience to agree with your point of view.
2. Explain in detail the effect of policies dealing with Native Americans had on their culture. Make sure to mention at least three specific policies and their effects.
3. Explain in a detailed essay how democracy and monarchy are similar and different. Make sure to compare and contrast them with regard to their structure, functions, and processes.
4. Write an informational essay explaining an important historical event. Include how that event was important in the past and how it is important to us in the present.

For average students, it is important that they plan their work using a graphic organizer. Teachers may actually look at the plan first to determine if students are on the right track before they take time writing an essay. See Chapter 3 for a generic graphic organizer for expository (nonfiction) writing and including persuasion.

Projects and Performances

Average students enjoy doing projects; however, they need to show the teacher that they are completing their work in a timely manner. In other words, the teacher should not assign the project and then check on how students have completed it on the due date. The teacher should plan checkpoints along the way.

Project or Performance Assessments

One of the best projects to assign average students is an inquiry-based self-selected project based on a topic within a unit of study. The teacher can assign the project as homework to supplement the work the students are doing in class to learn about the topic, or students can do it as an in-class experiential assessment process. Because it is inquiry-based, the teacher must make sure students understand how to cite sources and how to avoid plagiarism. Figure 4.21 is a generic research paper process.

Figure 4.21 Generic Inquiry-Based Project Syllabus

Inquiry-Based Project Syllabus

You can complete this project individually, with a partner, or with a small group (no more than five students to a group).

1. Choose a topic within our unit of study that you would like to explore in more depth. Due date:_____.

2. Find a minimum of _____(teacher decides the number based on time limits and level of students) sources. Sources might include primary sources, such as interviews and primary documents or secondary sources, such as accounts in encyclopedias and books written about the topic. Due date:_____

3. Take notes from your sources and think about how you might best show your knowledge of the topic. Go over the Project Rubric to make sure you understand how the teacher will evaluate your work. Due date:_____

4. Choose a product from this list or propose your own:
   ♦ An informational paper
   ♦ A children's book
   ♦ A creative story based on the information about the topic
   ♦ A pictorial explanation of the topic (drawings or photos), including written information about each picture
   ♦ A movement or dance based on the information you gather about the topic (requires a commentary explaining the movements)
   ♦ A live or filmed documentary or skit (with people or puppets) based on the topic
   ♦ A taped or live radio play or talk show based on the topic
   ♦ A PowerPoint presentation about the topic
   ♦ A three-dimensional display about the topic, including written commentary

5. Organize your information based on the project you choose and make a Works Cited page to show the sources you used to inform your project. Due date:_____

6. Explain your plan on the Project Proposal form (Figure 4.22). Due date:_____

7. Meet with the teacher to go over your plan. Due date:_____

8. Work on your project.

9. Sign up to present it and present it. Due date:_____

10. Accept feedback and evaluation from peers and from the teacher.

Note that there are checkpoints that are due along the way and that the syllabus includes several suggested products.

Figure 4.22. Project Proposal Template

Project Proposal

Your name(s):_____

Name of project:_____

Type of project (For example: film, PowerPoint presentation): _____

List sources of information:

1.

2.

3.

More:

_____ Check here if your Works Cited page is complete.

Learning objectives your project will address:

1.

2.

Time you need to present project: _____

Supplies and equipment you need for your project (for example, LCD projector, poster paper): _____

_____

Other comments:

When teachers meet with students, they should go over this form (Figure 4.22) with them to make sure they are on the right track. They should also make sure students have completed their Works Cited page correctly and that they understand the holistic rubric (Figure 4.23).

Figure 4.23. Holistic Rubric

Project Holistic Rubric

Level 1: Project information lacks depth and/or accuracy and does not show evidence of sufficient learning about the topic. It is poorly organized and lacks evidence of preparation. There is weak evidence of researched information supporting the project and much of it is well-known and/or copied from sources. The project lacks creativity, originality, and completeness. There is little to no audience awareness.

Level 2: Project information is superficial and at times inaccurate. There is some evidence of learning, but it is not extensive. The organization of the project does not add to its overall effect. There is little evidence of time spent to prepare it. Research is evident; however, it is superficial and overly dependent on prior knowledge and ideas that are elementary. The project shows some evidence of creativity, but that creativity is not well-aligned with the information or the learning objectives. Although there is some audience awareness, it is superficial.

Level 3: Project information is sufficient and accurate. The project clearly addresses the learning objectives and provides new ideas that go beyond students' prior knowledge and superficial information. Organization supports the overall effect of the project. Creativity is organic to the information the project presents. The project demonstrates a sense of audience awareness.

Level 4: Project information is extensive and accurate. The project supplies new ideas that go well-beyond students' prior knowledge and superficial information. The project shows evidence of a great deal of preparation and in-depth research. Organization enhances the delivery of the information. Creativity and originality are obvious and well-integrated with facts. The project shows a complex synthesis of the intended learning objectives. The project is highly successful in its connection with the audience.

Summary

Average students are the easiest to assess because most of them read at grade level and should respond to grade-level texts and activities. They should also have social skills that allow them to work in groups so that they might enjoy the learning process. Although they might be easier to assess, the teacher should still keep in mind that within the label, "regular," there is great variety of readiness, interests, and learning styles.

5

Enriched English and Social Studies Assessments

Academically gifted or advanced students have special assessment needs for which teachers should plan if they want to appropriately challenge them. As teachers begin to think about how to plan assessments for gifted or highly advanced students, they need to have a clear understanding of how these students think and behave.

This chapter shows teachers specific examples of differentiated assessment strategies that are leveled for students who are gifted or highly advanced. After providing an overview of these students' special needs, the chapter includes examples of preassessments, formative assessments, and summative assessments. For formative assessments there is information about the Differentiating Assessment: Six-Part Template. What follows is a thorough explanation of Part 1 of the Differentiating Assessment: Six-Part Template for students who may need enrichment.

Students Needs: Who Are These Students Who Need Enrichment Assessments?

To design effective assessments for gifted or highly advanced students, teachers need to keep in mind some of their particular strengths that might cause problems for teachers as they plan assessments for them. Figure 5.1 is a chart that shows how the social, emotional, and academic strengths of gifted or highly advanced students can cause problems for them and their teachers.

Figure 5.1. Social, Emotional, and Academic Strengths of Gifted or Highly Advanced Students

Strengths	Possible Resulting Assessment Issues
They learn information much more quickly than others and may in some cases actually be able to learn faster than some of their teachers.	They may become impatient with their peers or their teachers. They may get bored with the pace of the assessments if the teacher bases it on the needs of average students or his or her own learning pace.
They constantly ask questions and look for significance.	They may ask what appear to be inappropriate questions and may want to explore an issue in more depth than the rest of the class.
They are intrinsically motivated to learn.	They may resist the teacher's form of assessment, especially if he or she relies too much on extrinsic rewards.
They prefer assessments that allow them to show how they can solve problems, think abstractly, and synthesize information.	They are not as responsive to assessments that are standardized or that do not allow them to show their abilities.
They are highly concerned with fairness.	Assessments based on humanitarian concerns motivate them. They may challenge the teacher's fairness in some assessments.
They like to organize things and people.	They can seem bossy and critical of others when they are participating in a group assessment process.
They have sophisticated vocabularies.	They may use those words to manipulate or to challenge, which makes it more difficult for them to participate in assessments with average or at-risk students.
They have extremely high expectations of themselves.	They are often disappointed in themselves and others when they are not perfect. They may be obsessed with making the highest grades and scores on assessments. These expectations can interfere with their ability to participate in group assessments. The teacher may have to deal with their depression and sullenness if they do not achieve at the highest levels.
They are creative and like to do things in different ways.	They may not respond well to unimaginative assessments and may seem out of step with others.

They can concentrate intensely for long periods.	They may choose assessment projects that cause them to neglect everything but that assessment.
They are more sensitive to criticism than others are.	They may not respond well to any negative teacher or peer feedback for an assessment.
They are highly energetic and eager to use their minds.	They may appear hyperactive if the teacher requires them to endure assessments that bore them.
They are independent nonconformists.	They may prefer individualized assessments and may not prefer group assessments.
Their interests are varied, and they tend to use divergent thinking.	They may need teacher direction to stay focused on the goals of an assessment.

Adapted from http://www.kidsource.com/kidsource/content2/social_development_gifted.html (accessed July 30, 2008).

Knowing these things about gifted and highly advanced students, teachers must maintain sensitivity toward them if they want to give them the best chance of showing what they know.

How Learner Outcomes Differ for Gifted and Highly Advanced Students

Assessing gifted and highly advanced students differs quite a bit from assessing at-risk or average students. Figure 5.2 provides an excellent overview of social studies learning goals for average students as opposed to those for gifted or highly advanced students.

Figure 5.2. Learning Goals for Gifted or Highly Advanced Students

Average Students	*Gifted Students*
Comprehend the major concepts included in the unit	Evaluate diverse materials according to a set of criteria
Be familiar with the structural elements of the government	Create a self-selected product related to the important structural elements of democratic government
Develop an understanding of the parts of democratic government	Analyze and interpret the functions of politics, social structures, and economy on democratic government

These ideas were adapted from http://www.kidsource.com/kidsource/content/learner_outcomes.html (accessed July 30, 2008).

From this comparison it is obvious that assessments for gifted or highly advanced students are much more challenging, broader, and focused on higher-level thinking skills. Those who assess gifted and highly advanced students assume that these students can read and comprehend information above their grade level and that differentiating assessment is critical if the teacher wants to address their assessment needs.

English and Social Studies Examples of Preassessments

Anticipation Guide

Figure 5.3 is a social studies example of an Anticipation Guide (Herber, 1978) for gifted or highly advanced students. Notice that the vocabulary is higher level than for average or at-risk students. In addition, determining if the statement is true or false requires students to make some inferences.

Procedures

The way to conduct a lesson using this Anticipation Guide is as follows:

1. Hand out the Anticipation Guide as students enter the room.
2. Ask students to silently read the Anticipation Guide to decide if they agree (A) or disagree (D) with the statements listed on the guide.
3. Next, ask students to read the relevant sections of the textbook to find out if their ideas were correct.
4. After students have completed the guide, go over the answers as a class. Several of the statements will inspire debate because they are somewhat ambiguous and thought provoking.

Figure 5.3. Anticipation Guide for Gifted or Highly Advanced Students

Read the statements below and decide if you AGREE (A) or DISAGREE (D) with each statement. Write your answer in the left column under Anticipate. After you have learned about the topic, complete the right column under React. Notice what you have learned.

Anticipate	Statement	React
	1. Public education benefits the economy and growth of a state.	
	2. Individualism is required if states want to improve their economy.	
	3. In the early 1800s everyone in North Carolina had a right to a free education.	
	4. The heroism of Tsali is evident in the contemporary North Carolina culture.	
	5. The institution of slavery interfered with the spirit of democracy.	
	6. Cotton ruined North Carolina's economy.	
	7. Archibald Murphey made derogatory statements about the "common people" in North Carolina.	
	8. The main problem with the internal improvements legislated by the North Carolina General Assembly was that they were poorly designed.	
	9. Eastern politicians ruled North Carolina in the early and mid 1800s, and they still do.	
	10. When Archibald Murphey died in 1856, North Carolina was economically depressed and the masses were still living substandard lives.	

Key: 1. A; 2. D; 3. D; 4. A; 5. A; 6. A; 7. A; 8. D; 9. D; 10. A

Question Analysis

What follows is an analysis of *some* of the questions.

Question 3:   "In the early 1800s everyone in North Carolina had a right to a free education." This question requires students to think about the phrase "...had a right..." so that they make a decision about the spirit of the legislation and funding for educational programs in the 1800s. They must look at several factors to determine that the programs developed and funded by the North Carolina legislature did not in any way promote the "right" to a free education.

Question 4:   "The heroism of Tsali is evident in the contemporary North Carolina culture." To determine if this is a true statement, students must infer that Tsali's actions helped to make it possible for Native Americans to stay in North Carolina. They must also relate this new information to any prior knowledge they might have about current events related to Native American culture in North Carolina.

Question 6:   "Cotton ruined North Carolina's economy." Students must evaluate several pieces of information to determine if this is a true statement.

Questions 7 requires students to infer from a primary source.

Interview

Gifted or highly advanced students may enjoy the interview strategy. They usually have the social skills to stay focused on the topic and to take it seriously.

Procedures

Teachers give students an interview template or ask them to make their own interview format and then ask them to move around the room (the teacher could specify a certain amount of steps they should take to connect with their first interviewee) to find out what at least three students in the class already know about the topic. Students should report and then turn in their findings so that the teacher can get a better idea about what they already know. The teacher can teach these students to use "accountable talk." See Chapter 2 for an explanation.

English and Social Studies
Examples of Informal Assessments

Teachers can informally assess gifted and highly advanced students by using the methods described in Chapter 2. They might also use impromptu "multiple intelligences assessments" to determine if these students understand English or social studies concepts. A box of costumes, balls of string, hats, props, white paper, markers, glue sticks, a CD or tape player, and a keyboard or other instrument can be used in these assessments. When teachers introduce a new English or social studies concept, they might ask individuals, student partners, or small groups (no more than students to a group) to interpret these concepts for the class.

English Examples

1. Introduce the concept, "author's tone" and give students a short period of time (10–15 minutes) to use one of these intelligences: kinesthetic (dance, skit, commercial, puppet show); visual art (drawing, painting); or musical (song or rap) to show their understanding of "author's tone."

2. Have a box of author tones written on slips of paper and list those same tones on the board at the front of the room. As students enter the room, ask students to draw a tone out of the box. Instruct students to write a paragraph in the tone. Tell students to hand in their paragraphs as soon as they complete them. Then read the paragraphs students have written in the various tones. Students try to guess the tone. If at least one student guesses the tone, give that student an A. If no one guesses the tone, the student tries again to write a paragraph in that tone.

Social Studies Examples

1. Use the same process as item 1 in English examples with the concept "propaganda."

2. In groups, students learn about a specific propaganda technique (bandwagon, testimonial, glittering generalities, common man, etc.). They make a poster that represents one propaganda technique to share with the class. The class should guess which technique the poster represents.

Formative Assessments

Formative assessments allow teachers to determine if their students are learning what the teacher is teaching them. What follows are several examples of differentiated formative assessment strategies that will help the teacher enrich assessment for gifted or highly advanced students. For each assessment example, teachers will see examples of how to address Parts 2 through 5 of the Six-Part Template. The first part of this chapter covered Part 1—who are the students who need enrichment assessments—for all examples, and teachers can only complete Part 6 after they have implemented the assessment. Figure 5.4 is a review of the template for this process.

Figure 5.4. Differentiating Assessment: Six-Part Template

1. Students' Needs (described in detail)				
2. Curriculum				
Standard Course of Study (SCOS)	Essential Question (EQ)	Know	Understand	Do *(See MO below)*
3. Measurable Objective (MO)				
Introduction	Thinking Verb(s)	Product	Response Criterion	Content
4. Differentiation				
Readiness		Interests		Learning Styles
5. Assessment Procedures (listed by steps)				
6. Assessment Audit				

Examples of Formative Assessments

Differentiated Formative Assessments by Learning Styles

For the assessment strategies that follow, I use the differentiated and strategic categorizations discussed in Silver, Strong, and Perini (2007): mastery, understanding, self-expression, interpersonal, and four-style. I have adapted (including using alternative names for some similar concepts) their descriptions of these best practices, and I have focused on enriching the aspect of their usefulness as English and social studies assessment strategies for gifted and highly advanced students.

Mastery-Based Assessments

Direct Instruction

This strategy (Figure 5.5), which is updated from Madeline Hunter's mastery teaching strategies (Hunter, 2004; Marzano et al., 2001), allows for constant formative assessment during guided practice and independent practice.

Figure 5.5. Direct Instruction

Curriculum				
SCOS	**EQ:** How can we use "cover-read-recover-remember" to help us better understand a social studies text?	**Know**—how to use the cover-read-recover-remember strategy to read a social studies text, how to read for understanding, how to use the "fact trap" graphic organizer, how to identify main idea and supporting details in a social studies text.	**Understand** that using reading strategies can help us better understand a social studies text.	**Do**—use the cover-read-recover-remember and fact trap reading comprehension strategies with a social studies text, identify main ideas and supporting details *(see MO below)*.

Measurable Objective				
Introduction	**Thinking Verb(s)**	**Product**	**Response Criterion**	**Content**
Students will…	recall, recognize, organize, interpret, apply, differentiate, create, and produce	information organized by main ideas and supporting details	that demonstrates a thorough and accurate	comprehension of a social studies text.

Differentiation		
Readiness—teachers directly instruct students about how to use the process. They note students who need extra assistance	**Interests**—students make choices about how much text to cover each time and how they will cover the text	**Style**—auditory, visual, tactual, mastery

Procedures

When using this type of assessment with gifted or highly advanced students, the teacher must keep in mind that these students absorb information much more quickly and need less guided practice than at-risk or average students need; therefore, the teacher might replace guided practice with "facilitated" practice and troubleshooting.

Because this is an integrated assessment, the English and social studies teachers can provide the optimal learning experience if they plan the assessment together.

♦ Modeling—either the English or social studies teacher models a lesson, showing students how to cover-read-recover-remember to read and respond to a social studies text. As a direct instruction assessment process, teachers might use the following modeling strategies to explain the process:

- Visual—show students how to use a card or their hand to cover a section of the text (usually a long paragraph) on a topic in social studies. Showing them how to recover the same section as they remember what they have read, and demonstrate how they should record the main ideas and details they remember in a fact trap graphic organizer (see Chapter 2 for this organizer) helps visual learners. Students should draw their own fact traps for subsequent paragraphs because they will need a separate one for remaining paragraphs in the text (textbook chapter or other text).

- Oral—explain how students should cover a section of text, read it silently, and then record the main ideas and details in the fact-trap organizers. Model this process step by step for the first section of text and repeat modeling as needed.

- Tactual—ask students to use a card or their hands to interact with the text. This interaction addresses the needs of tactual learners.

♦ Assessment—collect the fact traps to assess students' ability to identify main ideas and details from a social studies text. Ask students to convert their fact traps into text outlines or to write a summary of the text. And, ask students to use their fact trap organizers as notes for an oral discussion of the text or to act as information for an extended writing assessment.

Reading for Meaning

One of the best strategies to assess whether gifted or highly advanced students have understood what they have read is to ask them to complete an inquiry-based project or research paper on a topic of their choice (Figure 5.6). By assigning these students to research a topic, they must read information on various levels, and they must synthesize their learning into a project or paper. This strategy comes from the work of Herber (1970) and Silver, Strong, and Perini (2007).

Figure 5.6. Inquiry-Based Research Paper, PowerPoint Presentation, and Speech

Curriculum				
SCOS	**EQ:** How can we use the research process to help us learn new information about a topic we choose?	**Know**—how to read new information for meaning, how to synthesize information from a variety of sources, how to use research to inform a paper from which to construct a PowerPoint presentation. Make a speech from a PowerPoint presentation.	**Understand** that deeply exploring a topic and writing about it requires certain forms and procedures.	**Do**—research, write a paper, plan a PowerPoint presentation, use the PowerPoint presentation to make a speech *(see MO below)*.

Measurable Objective				
Introduction	**Thinking Verb(s)**	**Product**	**Response Criterion**	**Content**
Students will...	interpret, generate, create, organize, and produce	a PowerPoint presentation, a research paper, and a speech	that meet the standards of the rubric that assesses	the information they provide about an English, social studies, or English/social studies integrated topic

Differentiation		
Readiness—syllabus with specific guidelines and checkpoints scaffolds assessment	**Interests**—students choose topic	**Style**—verbal/linguistic, artistic, visual, investigative, understanding, creative

Procedures

Step 1: Teachers hand out the syllabus and explain it to students. Figure 5.7 includes the syllabus for a research-based paper with a speech and Power-Point presentation.

Figure 5.7. Syllabus for Research Speech with PowerPoint Presentation

Name:_____ Due date: _____

1. *Choose* a topic from the following areas related to our unit of study:

   _____

   _____

2. Conduct research from a variety of sources (e.g., print and nonprint texts, artifacts, libraries, databases, computer networks, interviews with experts). Use your research to write a three-page paper from which to *create* a speech with an accompanying PowerPoint presentation. Use the information on the sheet titled "Big Six Steps for Conducting Research" (see Chapter 3) to guide the process of your research.

3. *Develop* an eight-slide PowerPoint presentation from your three-page paper. Slide 1 is the title and your name. Slide 8 is your "Works Cited" and "Fair Use" page. (See Figure 5.8, PowerPoint Presentation Rubric)

   ◆ *Make* an outline with proposed graphics to plan your PowerPoint presentation.

   ◆ Use graphics such as charts, diagrams, and graphs to enhance the communication of information.

   ◆ *Organize* your information in a logical sequence.

   ◆ Check for conventions such as spelling and grammar.

   ◆ Follow the rubric to assure a quality presentation.

4. Deliver a three-minute speech to the class using your PowerPoint presentation. (You can also allot time for questions and answers following your speech.) Do not read the speech to the class.

   ◆ You can use note cards to help you remember information, but your PowerPoint presentation should help you stay on topic. (You should *know* your information.)

Figure 5.8. PowerPoint Presentation Rubric

	No points	*Loss of sub-stantial points*	*Loss of some points*	*Maximum points*
Plan	Plan is incomplete	Plan is not complete, but includes a few of the assigned elements	Plan is complete	Plan shows exceptional and useful details
Organization of content	Content is presented in a random fashion that makes it difficult to follow	The sequencing of content shows a loss of focus that disrupts the flow of information	Logical sequencing of content	Logical, creative, and intuitive sequencing of content
Originality	The work is a minimal collection or rehash of other people's ideas and images. There is no evidence of new thought	The work is mostly a collection of other people's ideas and images. There is little evidence of new thought or inventiveness	The product shows some creative synthesis of research. Although it is based on a collection of other people's ideas, the words and images go beyond that collection to offer some new insights	The product shows significant evidence of creative synthesis of research. It demonstrates many new insights based on a depth of understanding based on logical conclusions and sound research
Subject knowledge	Subject knowledge is not evident. Information is confusing, incorrect or flawed	Subject knowledge is evident, but insufficient. Some information is confusing, incorrect or flawed	Subject knowledge is evident in much of the product. Information is clear, appropriate and correct	Subject knowledge is evident throughout (more than required). All information is clear, appropriate, and correct

	No points	Loss of sub-stantial points	Loss of some points	Maximum points
Graphical design	Graphics and/or pictures greatly interfere with the message	Graphics and pictures seem random and at times out of balance. There is little sense of harmony and attractiveness. Sometimes the design competes with the message rather than supporting it	Graphics and pictures combine with text to effectively deliver a strong message. Design techniques work well together	The combination of graphics, pictures and text is superior and develops communication that exceeds any message that may have been presented without that combination. This creative combination connects elegantly with the intended audience
Conventions	Presentation has four or more spelling errors and/or grammar errors	Presentation has three misspellings or grammar errors	Presentation has two misspellings and/or grammar errors	Presentation has no misspellings and/or grammar errors
Number and type of sources	No sources noted	Sources noted, but not in the correct form	Four sources noted	Four or more sources noted in the correct form and the correct types
Oral presentation	Speaker does not stick to time limit. Speech is often inaudible and indistinct. There is a negative or sarcastic attitude	Speaker does not stick to time limit. Speech is inaudible at times and indistinct. Speaker says "um" too much. There is a lack of conviction	Speaker sticks to time limit (is only off slightly), speaks distinctly and audibly with conviction	Speaker sticks closely to time limit, speaks distinctly and audibly with conviction. Develops a charismatic relationship with audience

Grading: You will receive a separate grade for the following parts of this assignment:

    I.   Paper

    II.   Speech

III. PowerPoint presentation

I. Maximum points for the **paper** are as follows:
    A. Outline (or other plan)   10 points
    B. Three-page paper (see rubric)   70 points
    C. Works Cited page   10 points (minimum two primary and two
        secondary sources)
    D. Note cards   10 points (minimum 15)
    Total   100 points

II. Maximum points for the **speech** are as follows:
    A. Sticking to time limit   50 points
    B. Speaking distinctly and audibly   20 points
    C. Speaking with conviction   20 points
    D. Developing a charismatic relationship with audience 10 points
    Total   100 points

III. Maximum points for **PowerPoint presentation** are as follows:
    A. Outline (plan)   10 points
    B. Organization   10 points
    C. Originality   20 points
    D. Subject knowledge   20 points
    E. Graphical design   10 points
    F. Conventions   10 points
    G. Number and types of sources   8 points
    H. Correct number of slides   10 points
    J. Catchy title   2 points
    Total   100 points

Evaluate the paper based on the holistic rubric shown in Figure 5.9.

Figure 5.9. Research Paper Holistic Rubric

1 (loss of more than 30 points)	2 (loss of 16–30 points)	3 (loss of between 1 and 15 points)	4 (no loss of points = 70)
Paper loses focus on the stated topic. Information is generally incomplete and inaccurate. Writer does not cite sources and may even plagiarize information. Information is disorganized and includes mostly common knowledge, quotes, or the writer's opinion. Ideas are not coherent or unified. Conventions errors make the paper difficult to read.	The writer loses the focus on the topic one or more times. Information lacks a sense of completeness and is often inaccurate. Writer does not use the correct method for citing sources in the body of the paper. Information is not well-organized and is often common knowledge, a string of quotes, or the writer's opinion. Writers' ideas are not generally coherent or unified. Conventions errors make understanding the writing difficult.	The writer consistently focuses on the stated topic. Information is complete and accurate. Writer sometimes does not use the correct method for citing sources in the body of the paper. Paper presents well-organized information that is most often beyond common knowledge or the writer's opinion. Writer presents ideas in a coherent and unified way. The writer has no more than six conventions errors.	The writer focuses on the stated topic, which is highly interesting to read. The writer presents information that is complete and accurately stated using the correct method for citing sources in the body of the paper. Paper presents well-organized information that extends beyond common knowledge or the writer's opinion. Writer presents ideas in a coherent and unified way. The writer has no more than three minor conventions errors.

Step 2: Teachers may want to consider the following sequence of assessments for using this reading for meaning assignment (Figure 5.10).

Figure 5.10. Sequence of Assessments

Schedule of Assessments of Students'
Achievement of Learning Goals Along the Way

	1 Start "Big Six" process I. Task definition	2 Media center II. Resource identification	3 Media center/computer lab III. Location and access	4 IV. Use of information Bring index cards to next class to begin taking notes. (teacher checks)
7 Computer lab for research	8 Computer lab for research	9 Computer lab for research	10 Computer lab for research	11 V. Synthesis Outline papers (teacher checks)
14 Finish outlining and organizing; begin writing papers (teacher checks outlines)	15 Write papers	16 Write papers	17 VI. Evaluation Peers edit papers (teacher checks); show powerful PowerPoint presentation (10–15 minutes)	18 Begin plan for PowerPoint presentation
20 Complete PowerPoint presentation plan; peers edit (teacher checks)	21 Computer lab to make PowerPoint presentations	22 Computer lab to make PowerPoint presentations	23 Computer Lab to make PowerPoint presentations; students sign up to make presentations (teacher checks)	24 Projects due; begin speeches
28 Continue speeches	29 Continue speeches	30 Finish all speeches		

Teachers can use the following instructions for taking notes (Figure 5.11), making an outline (Figure 5.12), organizing note cards (Figure 5.13, p. 151), writing the paper (Figure 5.14, p. 151), making a "Works Cited" and "Fair Use" slide (Figure 5.15, p. 152), and giving peer feedback to presenters (Figure 5.16, p. 152).

Figure 5.11.Taking Notes

How to Take Notes on Index Cards

1. Get a package of small index cards.
2. Make a "Works Cited" card for each source. Use MLA or APA format.
3. Take notes as follows:
    a. At the top of each card, make a parenthetical documentation notation (i.e., author's last name or shortened title if no author and page number—no comma).
    b. Write down *exactly* what the sources or the person you are interviewing says. You will paraphrase or synthesize the information into your paper but not on the card. You must be careful not to plagiarize (i.e., using the writer's exact words without quotes and parenthetical documentation or using the writer's thoughts without parenthetical documentation).
    c. Write *one* idea per card. You do not need to fill up the card. One to three sentences should be enough per card. You will need several cards per page of your paper.

Figure 5.12. Making an Outline

How to Make an Outline

Here is a general outline form for a research paper.

I. Introduction
    A. Catchy opening
    B. Topic statement
    C. Summary of main points
II. Main Idea 1
    A. Support 1
    B. Support 2
    C. Support 3 (minimum)
    D. Transition or draw a conclusion about the ideas
III. Main Idea 2
    A. Support 1
    B. Support 2
    C. Support 3

D. Transition or draw a conclusion about the ideas.

IV. Main Idea 3

A. Support 1

B. Support 2

C. Support 3

D. Transition or draw a conclusion about the ideas.

* You may include more main ideas, etc.

V. Conclusion

A. Restate the topic

B. Summarize main ideas

C. Draw a conclusion about your information, but do not add any new information.

Figure 5.13. Organizing Note Cards

How to Organize Your Note Cards in Preparation for Writing

1. Alphabetize your works cited cards.

2. Look at your outline and read each note card to determine under which Roman numeral the card will most likely fit. Put the Roman numeral at the top left-hand side of the card.

3. After you have decided where each card fits under each Roman numeral, decide where the card fits under the capital letters: A, B, C, etc. Put the appropriate *letter* next to the Roman numeral at the top left corner of the card.

4. Stack your cards in the order they will occur in the paper. The works cited cards go last. You can copy them in alphabetical order on a piece of paper to form your Works Cited page. Use rubber bands or large paper clips to separate the cards by their Roman numerals.

Figure 5.14. Writing the Paper

How to Write Your Paper

1. Whenever you use information from a note card, you must paraphrase or synthesize that information (put it in your own words or draw conclusions about it) and use parenthetical documentation to label each idea or group of ideas you use from your sources. Also, if you use the same source for an entire paragraph, you should only make the parenthetical notation at the end of that paragraph, not after every sentence.

2. Do not forget to use transitions to make your report coherent and do not leave any part out.

3. Read your paper carefully to edit for conventions errors.

Figure 5.15. Making a Works Cited and Fair Use Page

How to Make a Works Cited and Fair Use Page

1. Write *Works Cited* at the top of the page.

2. Use correct indentation and correct form to note your sources in alphabetical order.

3. For PowerPoint, make a works-cited slide and include a "Fair Use" statement at the end of it or make a separate slide.

Figure 5.16. Giving Peer Feedback to Presenters

Teachers should evaluate gifted or highly advanced students based on the provided rubrics, and they should ask peers to give student presenters feedback on their presentations based on that rubric.

1. Set up a visible timer to help students keep track of the time they are taking with their presentation.

2. Make sure to follow the order in which students signed up to present. If a student is not prepared to present, they lose points.

3. Provide each student with a small stack of small white strips of paper (i.e., enough for students to write feedback for each presenter).

4. Explain to students that after each student has presented, each member of the class will provide helpful feedback to them about their presentation. Stress the fact that this is not a grade and that only the teacher will be grading the presentation.

5. After each student presents, ask students in the audience to use the white strips of paper to score their presentation. They should include the student's name and a number for each category on the rubric.

6. Instruct the students who have completed a feedback paper to hold it up so that the students who have presented can get it. After the student has picked up all of the feedback papers, it is time for the next presenter.

Concept Attainment

This strategy includes assessing student's abilities to explore in depth what complex words might mean. Gifted or highly advanced students might learn a great deal about complex concepts using Jerome Bruner's (1973) process of "concept attainment" (Figure 5.17).

Figure 5.17. Concept Attainment

Curriculum				
SCOS	**EQ:** Why do I need to know about economics?	**Know**—how to define and use the concept of economics.	**Understand** that economics includes the development, management, and production of material wealth.	**Do**—use the process of concept development to learn about the concept of economics *(see MO below)*.

Measurable Objective				
Introduction	**Thinking Verb(s)**	**Product**	**Response Criterion**	**Content**
Students will…	generate, classify, compare, and organize	a list	that defines in detail	the concept of economics.

Differentiation		
Readiness—a teacher-led process scaffolds assessment	**Interests**—suspense and guessing create interest	**Style**—understanding, visual, investigative

Bruner's Concept Attainment—Social Studies Example

Procedures

Step 1: Select a social studies concept, such as economics. Next determine attributes that would fit under the "no" and the "yes" column. Make cards that are large enough for students to see from their desks, with one of the attributes listed on each card. Cards for this example would look like this and have tape on the backs so that they might be attached to the chart.

Production of material wealth

Positive examples are: management of material wealth, development of material wealth, production and management of material wealth for a country, production and management of wealth for a business or household.

Negative examples are: important uses of resources, results of time and talents, production of silver or gold, government control

Step 2: Hand out the following worksheet so that students might record what is happening on the board.

Concept Attainment

Student Worksheet　　　　Student's Name:_____

Yes	No

Step 3: Show the cards one at a time to the students. For the first card, "production of material wealth," say, "This card is a 'yes.'" For the next card, which could be "important uses of resources," say "This card is a 'no.'" Repeat this process until there are three examples on the board.

Step 4: Ask students to look at the "Yes" column and ask what the yes answers have in common. Tell students not to say out loud what they notice.

Step 5: Hold up the next three cards and ask students to say in which column they should go. Some students will get it, and others will not. Ask students to offer more examples, and prompt them to reveal the concept, "Economic pertains to the production, development, and management of the material wealth of a country, business, or household."

Step 6: Facilitate a discussion among students so that they might evaluate the process and talk about how they might apply it to future concept-attainment activities. Also, explore the concept of economics as it relates to your curriculum.

Self-Expression-Based Strategies

Inductive Learning

This is a brainstorming and predicting process that includes grouping, labeling, and generalizing to construct essential ideas. It is a wonderful assessment strategy to use if the teacher wants to challenge gifted or highly advanced students to explore essential concepts. Figure 5.18 is an English example of this assessment strategy.

Figure 5.18. Inductive Assessment—The Metaphor

Curriculum				
SCOS	**EQ:** What kinds of generalizations can we make about metaphors?	**Know**—how to form a generalization from information found through exploration of the construction and effect of metaphor.	**Understand** that exploring the parts of metaphors helps us better understand their construction and effects.	**Do**—create a metaphor for myself, identify metaphor written by others, generalizing from this experience *(see MO below)*.

Measurable Objective				
Introduction	**Thinking Verb(s)**	**Product**	**Response Criterion**	**Content**
Students will…	compare, explain, generate, attribute, implement, differentiate, and produce	a metaphor	that is sufficient and creative	about the student (him or herself).

Differentiation		
Readiness—guiding a process that is student-centered	**Interests**—students enjoy playing a game to discover new ideas about each other and to learn about a complex process	**Style**—self-expression, analytical, interpersonal, verbal-linguistic

Procedures

Step 1: Tell students that you will assess their ability to construct a metaphor and that through this inductive process they will gain a better understanding of the effect of metaphor in literature.

Step 2: Ask each student to take out a piece of paper to write a "metaphor for myself."

Step 3: Tell students that metaphors have three parts: tenor, vehicle, and shared characteristics. Explain that for this assessment, the student himself or herself is the "tenor," in other words, the subject that is being compared in the metaphor. Inform students that the purpose of the metaphor is to help an audience better understand the "tenor," and that during class, students will be revealing themselves through metaphor so that their classmates might better understand them..

Step 4: Ask each student to think of a "vehicle" to whom they might compare themselves. For example, a student might compare herself to a "puppy."

Step 5: Give students some think-time, and then ask them to think of five ways they are like the "vehicle." These ways are the "shared characteristics" the tenor (the student) has with the vehicle (the object of comparison). For example the girl who compares herself to a puppy might say that they share these characteristics: playful, cuddly, loyal, cute, and sweet. Teachers might use their own metaphor as an example.

Step 6: Ask students to write their shared characteristics to complete the metaphor. Tell students to hand in their metaphors as they complete them so that the class might play a "guessing game" in which they guess the "tenor" (the student) in the metaphor.

Step 7: When students have turned in all the metaphors, begin reading them aloud. Say for example, "This student is a puppy. She is playful, cuddly, loyal, cute, and sweet." Students raise their hands to guess who their classmate is who sees herself as a puppy. Students do not need to be graded on their guessing (they love to try to guess), however, students can be graded on the metaphors they write. (I have never known anyone to get less than an A+ on this assessment.)

Teachers might have a discussion with students so that they verbalize this generalization: Seeing how the parts of the metaphor work together helps students have a better understanding about the construction of metaphors and the purposes they serve.

Metaphorical Expression or Synectics

Gifted or highly advanced students can make great use of this form of assessment, which evaluates their ability to make meaning through a creative process of comparison called synectics (Figure 5.19). It was adapted from the work of Gordon (1961) and Silver, Strong, and Perini (2007).

Figure 5.19. Synectics

Curriculum				
SCOS	**EQ:** How is philosophy like a flower? How are flowers like philosophy?	**Know**—how to brainstorm connections between two unlike things to note metaphorical connections, create products that connect two unlike concepts.	**Understand** that we can compare two unlike concepts to help us deepen our understanding and knowledge of both of them.	**Do**—use the synectics process to deepen our understanding of two unlike concepts *(see MO below)*.

Measurable Objective				
Introduction	**Thinking Verb(s)**	**Product**	**Response Criterion**	**Content**
Students will…	generate, compare, create, and critique	metaphorical statements and creative products	that expand and enhance	understanding of philosophy.

Differentiation		
Readiness—guiding through a process scaffolds assessment	**Interests**—students brainstorm and draw from their own experiences and interests	**Style**—self-expression, analytical, creative

Synectics–Philosophy: Procedures

What follows is an English example showing how the teacher might assess gifted or highly advanced students using the synectics process. In each step, the teacher or designated student records the remarks of students as they brainstorm. The teacher makes it clear to students that no answer is silly or stupid and no one should criticize or make negative remarks about any remark.

Step 1: Introduce the topic: What is philosophy? Record all answers students might give about philosophy. Answers could be as follows: a set of beliefs related to a specific field of study; underlying theories; a system of thoughts; thinking about life, themes, religious ideas; scientific thinking; investigation of nature; wisdom; intellectual pursuit; a discipline that includes logic, ethics, aesthetics, metaphysics, and epistemology; a set of values to live by. Elicit deeper conceptualizations by asking questions, such as when do we think about philosophy? How do we develop our own philosophy? Give examples of philosophies, such as the philosophy of Confucius, the philosophy of Hume, or how a person might develop his own philosophy of life.

Step 2: Create an analogy: How is a philosophy like a flower? Both have shape, both are nonlinear, both have parts, both grow with time, both can be beautiful, there are many types of philosophies and many types of flowers, they both make life more interesting, they both have a center, and they both can be used in various ways. Ask students to think of how a philosophy might be like a flower. A sweet philosophy, a bitter philosophy, a bright philosophy, a beautiful philosophy, a philosophy that stings, a philosophy that needs sunlight and one that needs shade, a philosophy that has many parts or one that has fewer parts, and a philosophy that we can digest and one that is hard to digest.

Step 3: Ask students to draw one of the analogies on a sheet of paper. For example students could draw a philosophy that needs light or one that needs shade, a philosophy that is beautiful, a philosophy that has many parts or few parts.

Step 4: Students explore as a whole class discussion or with a partner how some of the words they have listed seem to be in conflict: for example, "light" and "shade" show conflicting environments for growth; "few parts" and "many parts" show conflicting organizations; "bitter" and "sweet" show conflict in palatability.

Step 5: Create a new analogy. Students propose new analogies and vote on one based on their drawings and performances. For example, students could decide that the best new analogy compares bitter to sweet philosophy in terms of how it might be received and understood (digested).

Step 6: Look for words or phrases that "redefine" philosophy and that make learning about them a richer experience. For example, when we read philosophies or create our own, we can see how they might be well received or poorly received or how the philosophy might be simple or complicated. Also, when we see flowers we can think of them as representatives of the concept of philosophy. Here are some suggestions for assessment products:

- Create a flower arrangement with real or constructed flowers. Write a commentary explaining the philosophy each flower represents and why you arranged the flowers as you did.

- Create a picture of a philosophical flower garden. Include some of the major philosophies that inform Western and Eastern cultures represented as flowers.

- Write a report on an important philosophy and how it blooms in modern times to address a contemporary psychological or sociological issue.

- Create a graphic organizer that analyzes in detail how philosophy and flowers are similar and different.

- Create a film using flowers as symbolic props to show the way a philosophy might address a current social problem.

Interpersonal-Based Assessments

Interpersonal-based assessments use students' natural inclination to help each other and work together; therefore, gifted or highly advanced students enjoy these unless they are social isolates. In that case teachers may need to use curriculum compacting or some other individualized contracting with them.

Jigsaw

This cooperative learning assessment (Figure 5.20, p. 160), adapted from Aronson et al. (1978), works well with gifted or highly advanced students, who can use this activity with very little practice or teacher modeling.

Figure 5.20. Jigsaw

Curriculum				
SCOS	**EQ:** How did European exploration of the Americas affect Europeans, Native Americans, and Africans?	**Know**—how to teach others about various historical events, information about the effect of various historical events on three cultures, how to work effectively in a group.	**Understand** that European exploration of the Americas had a major effect on Europeans, Native Americans, and Africans.	**Do**—read about specific historical events, plan how to teach the information to peers, teach the information, and assess the learning *(see MO below)*.

Measurable Objective				
Introduction	**Thinking Verb(s)**	**Product**	**Response Criterion**	**Content**
Students will...	summarize, compare, explain, organize, differentiate, plan, and produce	teaching materials	that adequately and accurately	explain the effect of European exploration of the Americas on three cultures: Europeans, Native Americans, and Africans.

Differentiation		
Readiness—teacher-guided process scaffolds assessment	**Interests**—working in a group to learn together, choosing how to teach a topic	**Style**—interpersonal, investigative, visual and auditory, verbal/linguistic

Procedures for Jigsaw—The Meeting of Three Cultures

Here is an example of using Jigsaw as a way to assess students' learning a social studies topic. Teachers should use this activity as they explore how European exploration of the Americas brought together three cultures: Europeans, Native Americans, and Africans. Assign the following subtopics: (1) the exploration activities of the English, (2) the exploration activities of Spain and Portugal, (3) how the Native Americans reacted to the exploration and colonization of their land, and (4) how the Africans were affected by the beginnings of slavery.

Step 1: Put each student in a home group and ask them to number off one through four. If there are an uneven number of students, make a group of five. There may be several groups of four or five.

Step 2: Assign students who are number 4 (and 5) to read about the exploration activities of the English, students who are number 3 to read about the exploration activities of Spain and Portugal, students who are number 2 to read about how Native Americans reacted to the exploration and colonization of their land, and assign students who are number 1 to read about how Africans were affected by the beginnings of slavery.

Step 3: Instruct students to move to a 1 table, a 2 table, a 3 table, or a 4 table. Tell students at each table that they should read their assignment and complete some products with which to teach their home group about their topic. Structure this activity by giving students blank white paper or poster paper, cards, and markers so that they might construct some flashcards or posters that teach about their topic. Ask students to make a five-problem quiz to test their home group members' knowledge of their topic. Students should make a quiz for each member of their home group. The groups should have four or five members.

Step 4: When students return to their home groups, they should take turns teaching that group about their type topic.

Step 5: Collect and evaluate student-made materials and quizzes. Test students on the information with a summative standardized test or a writing assignment.

Community Circle

This strategy, adapted from Silver, Strong, and Perini (2007), is a way to allow students a chance to voice their thoughts, feelings, and values. It is not to be confused with a Socratic seminar, which assesses what students might have learned about a topic. Figure 5.21 (p. 162) includes suggested English and social studies topics for Community Circle.

Figure 5.21. Topics for Community Circle

Curriculum				
SCOS	**EQ:** See list of possible questions.	**Know**—how to connect feelings and thoughts to high-level open-ended topics.	**Understand** that students' feelings and thoughts are valuable in the classroom.	**Do**—express feelings, thoughts, and values in a safe environment *(see MO below)*.

Measurable Objective				
Introduction	**Thinking Verb(s)**	**Product**	**Response Criterion**	**Content**
Students will…	explain, summarize, and produce	oral responses	that are on topic, honest, and complete	about a variety of English and social studies topics.

Differentiation		
Readiness—facilitation of the process scaffolds assessment	**Interests**—students connect with their own feelings and generate their own thoughts about highly interesting and relevant topics	**Style**—open-ended, creative, interpersonal

Procedures

This process is more like a classroom meeting during which the teacher might assess concerns students are having about an issue in class, or the teacher could use it to assess students' prior knowledge and understanding of an English or social studies topic. The process works best for most students if they are in a circle. What follows are some possible English and social studies topics that gifted or highly advanced students might enjoy discussing:

- ◆ English
  - How does literacy help us gain access to the power code of society?
  - What would the world be like without reading?
  - How is literature an art form?
  - Why is it important to be able to express yourself clearly and persuasively in writing?
  - How does analyzing literature relate to problem solving in the real world?

◆ Social Studies

- Why is it important to solve social issues in humanistic ways?

- Why should it bother us that people from foreign cultures experience oppression?

- How is our American way of life at risk?

- What is the most destructive social problem in our country?

- What can a student do to promote world peace?

Q-Space

For the Community Circle or to deepen any discussion, the teacher might use a strategy called Q-Space (developed by Strong, Hanson, & Silver, 1995):

- ◆ Question
- ◆ Silence and wait time
- ◆ Probing
- ◆ Accepting
- ◆ Clarifying and correcting
- ◆ Elaborating

Four-Style Assessment

Seminar, Socratic Seminar, Circle of Knowledge, or Dialogic Learning

This is a method of assessing students orally, and it works extremely well with gifted or highly advanced students; it seems to be tailor-made for them. They thrive on it, and most of the time teachers do not have to be concerned with assigning seats. They may want to move students if they talk to their neighbors too much. Figure 5.22 (p. 164) provides a suggested seminar on Internet ethics.

Figure 5.22. Seminar on Internet Ethics

Curriculum				
SCOS	**EQ:** Can the Internet have harmful effects on our society?	**Know**—how to connect feelings and thoughts to high level open-ended topics, how to express themselves orally.	**Understand** that the Internet can have serious and potentially harmful effects on our society.	**Do**—express feelings, thoughts, and values in a safe environment, connect personal feelings with a specific text, learn to support opinions with detailed information *(see MO below)*.

Measurable Objective				
Introduction	**Thinking Verb(s)**	**Product**	**Response Criterion**	**Content**
Students will...	explain, summarize, produce, exemplify, attribute, and generate	oral responses	that are respectful, of others, thorough, accurate, and reference the text	about effects of technology on society.

Differentiation		
Readiness—facilitation and practice scaffolds assessment	**Interests**—students connect with their own feelings and generate their own thoughts about this highly interesting and relevant topic	**Style**—open-ended, creative, interpersonal

Seminar Assessment—General and Technology Example

Unlike the community discussions described previously, this strategy allows the teacher to assess academic learning that is "tied to a text." The following is an example of a seminar experience for gifted or highly advanced students, starting with a process useful to both English and social studies and finishing with a social studies example.

Procedures

Step 1: Identify an above–grade-level and/or on–grade-level interesting text for the students to read. This text could be in students' textbooks or one taken from another source such as the Internet. Ask students to read this selection and annotate it as best they can (meaning making notes on the side with questions and other ideas). Their annotations could include responses to a specific theme or question. For example, ask students to note places in the text that point to ethical issues involved in technological advances.

Step 2: Tell students that during the next class they will be participating in a seminar discussion of this text and that everyone should bring at least two questions to help with the discussion. Teach students to write Level 2 and 3 type questions (see "How to Write Seminar Questions" in Chapter 3).

Assume that students will write their questions for homework; however, check for understanding by asking students to share some of their ideas. Writing the questions perfectly the first time is not critical. As the class repeats the process, they will write increasingly sophisticated discussion questions.

Step 3: For the next class, arrange the desks in a circle.

Step 4: Join the circle and explain the rules and expectations that you have also posted in the room or held for students to see. Another idea is to hand out a copy of the rules and expectations to students in addition to the posting of them (see Seminar Rules and Expectations in Chapter 3).

Step 6: To finish the seminar, give shy or reluctant students a chance to speak. Give these students a "parting shot" question that is relatively easy to answer.

To grade a seminar, use the oral assessment grading grid shown in Chapter 2.

The following steps can be used for a technology assessment.

Step 1: Ask students to read an essay called "The Internet, Computer Games, and Morality" (Wu, 1999) from "Ethics, Technology and Science," which is an award-winning ThinkQuest. Note: Teachers can find a wealth of resources that are sure to interest gifted or highly advanced students on the ThinkQuest.org website. Their library of award-winning ThinkQuests is worth checking out at www.thinkquest.org/library.

Step 2: Explain to students how to write Level 2 and 3 questions. Here are some Level 2 examples for this essay:

- Do violent video games negatively affect children and teenagers?
- Why is the Internet anarchistic?
- How can the Internet be unethical?
- Which examples of Internet immorality are most dangerous?

Here are some Level 3 examples:

- What does the Internet teach us about responsible social science?
- How could the Internet be useful to promote morality?
- Is morality always a choice?
- How might parents protect their children from Internet immorality?
- Which aspects of the Internet are most threatening to our society?

Follow the general rules and expectations for the remainder of this process.

Mini-Seminar: An Adaptation of Whole-Class Seminar

To offer a chance for even more intense conversation about a topic, teachers can divide the class in half, into medium-sized groups, or into groups of four or five students. Note: Teachers should only use this method after students have practiced the whole-class method of seminar discussion. To use this adapted version of seminar, teachers should take the following steps:

Step 1: Choose the content and a method of developing questions for seminar. Supply the questions or require students to generate them.

Step 2: Decide how to group the students. Here are some suggestions:

- Divide the class in half. Have one group of quiet and perhaps shy students and another group of more outgoing and verbal students.
- Divide the class into thirds based on learning styles.
- Form heterogeneous groups of four or five, making sure each group has a strong student leader and a good mix of abilities.

Step 3: Make sure each group has a leader and a recorder. The students can elect these leaders, or you can appoint them.

Step 4: Give these instructions:

1. The group leader will keep the discussion going. He or she will ask questions and allow others to ask them.

2. The recorder should record on a sheet of paper the names of each member of the group leaving three or four spaces between the names. The recorder's job is to put a slash mark (/) each time a student makes a comment. It is the recorder's responsibility to make sure all students get credit for contributing to the conversation.

3. I will grade you each on the number of comments you make that add to the conversation.

4. Are there any questions? You may begin.

Step 5: Circulate constantly to assure that the discussions are going smoothly. Encourage groups to give each student a chance to talk. Most gifted or highly advanced students take this process seriously and participate well.

Step 6: Evaluate this assessment by counting the number of comments each student makes in comparison with other members of the group. For example some groups have students who make detailed remarks; therefore, their recorder may have recorded fewer comments. Teachers can tell the style of the group and adjust the grading to match it.

(Note: With all of these formative assessments, it is important to rotate them so that students may have an opportunity to experience each type of assessment.)

Summative Assessments for Gifted or Highly Advanced Students

Most textbooks provide summative assessments for teachers to use with gifted or advanced students; however, they should find assessments for gifted or highly advanced students that challenge them beyond what average or at-risk students might be able to do. The critical issues for summative assessments for gifted or highly advanced students are as follows:

♦ Teachers should not require them to do more questions than other students do, but their questions might be more open-ended and detailed.

♦ Sometimes convergent test questions do not allow gifted or highly advanced student to do what they do so well, and that is divergent thinking. For example, some gifted and highly advanced student do poorly on "one-right-answer" tests because they overanalyze and might see too many possibilities to settle on the one-right-answer the test-maker decided was correct.

Constructing Summative Assessments for Gifted or Highly Advanced Students

See Chapter 3 for examples of summative assessments with a style that is similar for gifted or highly advanced students. The content should be more challenging, and the wording of the question stem should move as high up the thinking taxonomy as the question style will allow. Multiple-choice questions may be the easiest to make higher level.

Gifted or highly advanced students may best be tested using extended writing (essay) samples or projects mainly because it is much easier to make them higher level. For example, according to the New Bloom's Taxonomy (Anderson et al., 2001), "creating" is the highest level of thinking.

Teachers can find enrichment essay prompts and project ideas in their textbooks or online. For almost every unit of study, teachers might go to www.Google.com to find a wealth of assessment resources. In Northey (2005), I include a "Multiple Intelligence and Problem-Type Matrix." Teachers should note that for gifted or highly advanced students, the more open-ended the problem type, the better some of them will respond. My book, *The Democratic Differentiated Classroom* (Waterman, 2007), shows how I worked with gifted and highly advanced students using student-led unit planning. Many of the gifted students in my class worked amazingly hard on the projects they designed based on a theme the class chose. From that theme, they used a project to answer a specific essential question that they chose to address.

One of the most exciting processes related to assessment is the development of the "consensus rubric." Gifted or highly advanced students know how to set criteria and standards for their projects so that the teacher can evaluate them based on the ideas they find important. Democratic differentiation is organic to differentiating instruction for gifted or highly advanced students; therefore, teachers might want to explore the model in more detail. See Chapter 4 for writing and project templates that work well for both gifted or highly advanced and average students such as the following:

♦ Writing organizers

♦ Generic inquiry-based project syllabus

♦ Project proposal

♦ Project holistic rubric (or better yet, allow students to create a consensus rubric as mentioned earlier)

Extended-Writing Assessments

One of the best ways to assess gifted or highly advanced students' learning is to assign an extended-writing assessment.

Procedures

Figure 5.23 includes suggested English and social studies topics for writing assignments categorized by "modes" of writing.

Figure 5.23. English and Social Studies
Topic for Extended Writing Assessments

Writing Mode	Content	Prompt ideas
Descriptive	English	♦ Choose a character from a novel or story you have read. Describe the character in detail so that we can see what he or she looks like. ♦ Choose a novel or short story with an interesting setting. Describe that setting so that reader can see what it looks like.
	Social Studies	♦ Create a small planet and vividly describe what it looks like. Make sure to use these social studies terms in your description: landforms, topography, government, economy, climate. ♦ (For any social studies content) write a thorough and detailed description of_____(supply the topic, such as "the first colony in America").
Narrative	English	Write a story that includes the following: (1) a basic situation (exposition—includes characters, setting, and what is going on); (2) a problem, which includes conflict and rising action; (3) a climax (determining when the main conflict is solved); and (4) a resolution (which is what happens after the major conflict is solved).
	Social Studies	Write a story that includes social studies vocabulary and information from any social studies unit of study. For example: Write a story that fictionalizes the "The Lewis and Clark Expedition." Use vocabulary terms listed in your textbook and information from several sources including your textbook. Make sure your story has interesting characters, setting, conflict, and resolution.

Writing Mode	Content	Prompt ideas
Expository/ Informative	English	For any concept, students can write a detailed explanation of the processes involved. The teacher should show students how to organize their writing using the following: 1. Organization—introduction, body, conclusion (IBC) form; 2. Sufficient information using the following: (a) main ideas, (b) supporting details that provide examples, and (c) conclusions drawn from those ideas; 3. Appropriate beginning and ending; and 4. Reasonable control of grammar, usage, and spelling. Prompts could include asking students to show causes and effects or to write an extended definition, for example, "write a composition that thoroughly explains the internal conflict in a story or novel."
	Social Studies	For any social studies topic, the student can write a detailed explanation. The teacher should use the information presented above as a general outline, for example, "write a composition explaining the effects of landforms on a specific culture."
Persuasive/ Argumentative	English	For any English topic, students might write to convince the audience to agree with their perspective, to recommend something, or to suggest a specific solution to a problem, for example, "choose a novel with an ambiguous ending. Convince your reader that your description of the ending is the best interpretation."
	Social Studies	Numerous social studies topics lend themselves to persuasive prompts. The teacher can actually encourage students to take a stand on an issue that affects their community and support their writing letters to the editor or to community leaders in an attempt to leverage real change.

Twenty-First–Century Projects

Gifted or highly advanced students are probably more connected to this century in terms of technology skills than are many of their teachers. It is doing a disservice to these twenty-first-century students if teachers do not allow them to (or show them how to) use the latest technological advances that might be useful as summative assessment vehicles.

Most teachers have some knowledge of allowing students to use PowerPoint presentations as a way to show what they have learned about an English or social studies topic; however, not as many teachers allow students to make other technology-based products such as films or podcasts. With any multimedia project for which students gather pictures, music, or text from outside sources, comes the issue of copyright. Make sure that students understand copyright laws, especially the concept of "fair use." There are several sources of copyright policies. Teachers should choose the one or ones that their students will understand.

Filmmaking

Figure 5.24 shows how to use filmmaking as a summative assessment for gifted or highly advanced students and Figure 5.25 (p. 172) is the syllabus for such a project.

Figure 5.24. Filmmaking Project

Filmmaking Procedures

What follows is a general outline for how to set up a filmmaking project:

Step 1: Choose a topic or allow students to choose a topic based on their interests and the material from the unit of study (including essential understandings and questions). Allow students to work alone, with a partner, or in a small (no more than four students) group.

Step 2: Provide students with a rubric template on which to develop criteria for a quality film.

Step 3: Group students according to the topics they have chosen. These groups view a student-made film that provides an excellent example and one that has problems. Teachers can find a wealth of these films from www.studentfilms.com or www.studentfilmmakers.com. There are also some excellent student film examples on www.myhero.com.

Step 4: The whole class discusses issues of quality and lack of quality. Following this discussion, students work together to create a rubric that reflects the discussion and their ideas.

Step 5: Collect these rubrics and consolidate them into one "class rubric."

Step 6: During the next class, share that rubric with the class and hand out the syllabus (Figure 5.25).

Step 7: Provide each person, partnership, or group, a template and directions for how to construct a storyboard for a film. A good resource for this information is www.storycenter.org/memvoice/pages/tutorial_3.html (which has a template and directions for completing a storyboard). If you do not like this source of information, you might google "storyboards" to find other resources.

Step 8: Use a student-made short film, which you analyze frame by frame to show students how the creator of the film might have used a storyboard. The class follows along recording the same information on their sheets of paper.

If you have time, show another very short film so that students might practice the process of making a storyboard on their own.

Step 9: With partners or in small groups, students create a rubric for evaluating their storyboards, and as with the film rubric, construct and produce a composite rubric from among their responses.

Step 10:   Students can work either in class or at home to design their storyboards and then their films. Check on their progress periodically and encourage them to make an appointment with the teacher or media specialist to work on editing the film.

Step 11:   You or the media specialist should help students edit their films using a film-editing program.

Step 12:   Students present and receive feedback from their peers and a grade from the teacher.

Figure 5.25. Filmmaking Syllabus

1. Choose a topic that addresses an important aspect of our unit of study. Due date: _____.

2. Either work alone, find a partner, or work with a small group (no more than four students). Submit your plan by: _____.

3. Create a storyboard for your film. Date due: _____.

4. Create your film. Date due: _____.

5. Make an appointment with the media specialist to get help editing your film. Date of appointment: _____.

6. Sign up to present your film.

7. Present the film on this date: _____.

8. Grade: _____.

Comments:

Podcasting

Podcasting is a relatively new and exciting way for gifted or highly advanced students to show what they have learned from a unit of study.

Procedures

If you are interested in allowing your students to use a podcast as a summative assessment, familiarize yourself with this technology, or if you are not inclined to learn how to do it yourself, allow your tech-savvy students to use it.

Podcasting involves creating a series of digital-media files that the student can distribute over the Internet using syndication feeds for playback on portable media players and computers. A podcast differs from other digital media formats because podcasters can syndicate their work, others can subscribed to it, and it is easy to download when the podcaster needs to add new content. The podcaster can add new content using an aggregator or feed reader capable of reading feed formats such as RSS or Atom. Figure 5.26 provides the steps for teaching students to create a podcast.

Figure 5.26. Podcasting Project

These steps were adapted from www.podcastingnews.com/article/How-to-podcast.html (accessed December 3, 2008).

Step 1: Tell students they will be creating a podcast. Ask students what they already know about podcasting to find out how to differentiate the instruction.

Step 2: Show at least one example of an excellent podcast and one of a poor podcast, and as with the filmmaking unit, the students should create a rubric for evaluating both the podcast plan and the actual podcast.

Step 3: Students may work alone, with a partner, or in a small group to create the content for their show. Content could include interviews, music, commentary, or anything the students find interesting. Use a specific planning format or allow students to determine their own.

Step 4: After assessing the students' podcast plan, help them record the audio using Audacity, an open-source, cross-platform, and free resource that allows students to mix multiple audio files.

Step 5: Students should save their finished audio show at maximum quality in the native format of their audio application. Saving this allows students to edit or reuse their recording to have a good version.

Step 6: Once the students have their completed audio content, they need to convert their file to MP3 format. Using MP3 format allows universal access to the podcast. Students should use the minimum bit rate that provides good results. Here are some suggested settings:

48–56k mono—sermons, audio books, talk radio

64k+ stereo—music, music and talk combinations

128k stereo—good quality music

Students should save their work with a .mp3 file extension. (Students and teacher might read the article "Saving MP3 Files for Podcasting," available at www.podcastingnews.com/article/saving-MP3-files-for-podcasting.html.)

Step 7: Students save their MP3 files on the webserver to test them with an MP3 player. The files can go anywhere on the site, but students might want to put all of them into one directory so they might be easy to find.

Step 8: Students next create a podcast news feed. These news feeds are RSS files that describe the podcast along with information for each show. An RSS file is a text file that links students to their MP3 file. Student can read about RSS at http://www.podcastingnews.com/articles/Understanding_RSS_Feeds.html.

Step 9: Students can use any text editor to create an RSS news feed, however, most podcasters use blogging programs or other applications that automatically generate news feeds. If students use a blogging tool that lets them reference "enclosures," they should create an item for each MP3 file they publish, and they should use an URL of audio content as their enclosure. If the blogging tool does not support enclosures, students may edit their RSS file with any text editor to add the enclosure tag. Here is an example from the Trade Secrets podcast news feed:

TS20041107.mp3" length="49885056" type="audio/mpeg"/>

Students should understand that RSS news feeds normally show news items that contain a title, link, and description. Each item in a news feed provides meta-information about a URL on the Web. For a podcast news feed, each item describes the content of an audio file that is referenced by the enclosure URL. Students should save their RSS file with a .rss or .xml extension. Students should have one news feed that holds all of their recent work from newest to oldest.

Step 10: Students should transfer their podcast RSS file to the webserver in the same way they would save any other content. They should validate this using an online RSS validator. If the podcast news feed is valid, it is ready to be published to the World Wide Web. Students might develop a podcast logo and should publish their work on a Podcast Directory.

Step 11: Students should present their podcasts to the class, receive feedback from their peers and a grade from their teacher.

Other Useful Summative Assessments for Gifted or Highly Advanced Students

Gifted or highly advanced students thrive on novelty and chances to make choices about how they show what they know. What follows is a short list of some of the best summative assessments for these students:

♦ In-school field trip

Allow students to develop classroom centers that address the content of a unit of study in English, social studies, or English/social studies. These centers could be a demonstration, a speaker, an exhibit, a game, or a simulation. Students plan and develop these centers and offer them to the rest of the school as a field trip within the walls of the school. Teachers supply students with field-trip journals or assignment sheets in which they record their learning and their reflections.

♦ Book study

Teachers identify books that have social issues as their themes and ask students to read them to discover specific content. Students can write about these books, make an artistic project, or have a seminar discussion. The whole class could read the book together, or students might select their own books to read.

♦ Trial simulation

Teachers can use a work of literature or social problem that might involve a crime. For example, the class could try a business that is exploiting or oppressing a group of people. Teachers can take the following steps to simulate a trial in the classroom.

Step 1: Ask students how they stand on the issue. The issue must have two distinct sides that students might take in a somewhat equal manner. Because this is a role-playing event, assign the following roles: three defense lawyers, three prosecution lawyers, a defendant, witnesses, and jury members. The teacher is the judge.

Step 2: Present the role assignments as follows:

- Lawyers: Develop the case in writing including generating the questions to ask the witnesses and opening and closing statements. Develop props such as pretend x-rays and other supporting artifacts to support the case.

- Witnesses: Write a brief description of your characters and your stance on the issue; role play being questioned on the witness stand. Witnesses can use costumes and props (e.g., crutches and bandages).

- Jury: While the lawyers and witnesses are developing their piece of the process, the jury writes their stand on the issue (one member should be the foreman).

Step 3: Set the class up as much like a courtroom as possible. The judge (teacher) begins the process. Ask the prosecution to make their opening statement (make a time limit, such as 3 minutes) and to question their witnesses. Next, allow the defense to make their case. After both have presented their cases, the prosecution makes a closing statement, and then the defense makes theirs. Finally the jury votes using a silent ballot on the fate of the defendant, and the foreman announces the results.

Summary

Gifted or highly advanced students can enjoy working with others or alone to solve open-ended problems and to respond to appropriate challenges. To differentiate assessment for them, teachers must understand them as a group and as individuals.

It may be challenging to construct assessments that motivate them and encourage them. The most successful assessments for these kinds of students is to ask students to think, evaluate, and create at high levels.

6

Putting It All Together

In this chapter the teacher will see how to use the Differentiating Assessment: Six-Part Template process with a composite secondary teacher's classes. The units of study will be as follows for this composite roster of students:

1. An English unit differentiated by readiness using "tiering"
2. A social studies unit differentiated by learning styles using student choices
3. An integrated English and Social Studies unit differentiated by interests and reading readiness

For these units of study, teachers will see examples of how to apply the Differentiating Assessment: Six-Part Template to implement differentiated assessment. Figure 6.1 is a review of using the six parts of planning differentiated assessment, and Figure 6.2 (p. 178) is the Differentiating Assessment: Six-Part Template.

Figure 6.1. Six Parts of Planning Differentiated Assessment

1. **Students' Needs:** Who are the students in terms of: (a) readiness, (b) interests, and (c) learning and thinking styles, and what do they already know about the topic?

2. **Curriculum:** What enduring essential knowledge (EEK) [expressed as essential questions (EQs)] do these students need to know, understand, and do (KUD)? Note that the measurable objective(s) is listed separately in Part 3 but is also included under Curriculum.

3. **Measurable Objectives:** How will the teacher measure that learning?

4. **Differentiation:** How should the teacher differentiate the assessment to meet the learning needs of students?

5. **Procedures:** What procedures will the teacher follow to implement the assessment?

6. **Assessment Audit:** How will the teacher evaluate the alignment of the assessment(s) and procedures so that he or she has a clear picture of what each student knows, understands, and can do related to the content?

Figure 6.2. Differentiating Assessment: Six-Part Template

1. Students' Needs (described in detail)				
2. Curriculum				
Standard Course of Study (SCOS)	**Essential Question (EQ)**	**Know**	**Understand**	**Do** *(See MO below)*
3. Measurable Objective (MO)				
Introduction	**Thinking Verb(s)**	**Product**	**Response Criterion**	**Content**
4. Differentiation				
Readiness		**Interests**		**Learning Styles**
5. Assessment Procedures (listed by steps)				
6. Assessment Audit				

Part 1: Students' Needs

Unless they have a special needs roster, most middle or high school teachers have between four and six classes of students for whom to plan units of study. They often have between 80 and 150 or more student contacts. These students will naturally have varied learning skills and deficiencies, interests, and styles of learning; therefore, to provide the best assessments, the teacher will need to plan all units of study using differentiated assessment. The usual secondary class roster will have some of the following general types of students:

- ♦ Learning disabled (LD) in reading, writing, math, or other (motivated or unmotivated)
- ♦ English language learner (ELL) for whom English is a second language (motivated or unmotivated)
- ♦ At-risk learners several levels below grade (motivated or unmotivated)
- ♦ Average ability, on grade level (motivated or unmotivated)
- ♦ Gifted or highly advanced (motivated or unmotivated)
- ♦ Others

The most challenging of the students are those who are unmotivated at any level. *The examples will show how teachers might plan unit assessments for classes that include all of the types previously listed (Part 1 will be the same for all three examples).*

Novel Study: Literacy Readiness Using Tiering

This unit (Figure 6.3) is an adapted version of Literature Circles (Daniels, 1994). The teacher differentiates the unit by content based on readiness levels; in other words, it is tiered to address various students' reading levels. Teachers do not differentiate the process because all groups use the same one. Teachers do differentiate the project because that allows students to choose a project that matches their learning style.

Figure 6.3. Novel Study—Literacy Readiness Using Tiering

Students' Needs (see above for a description of students' needs)				
Curriculum				
SCOS	**EQ:** How might we deepen our understanding of longer works of literature by discussing them in a structured way with our peers?	**Know**—how to share the responsibility of discussing a longer work of literature (fiction or nonfiction); how to be a discussion leader; an illustrator, a passage pointer, or a vocabulary builder; how to create a project that demonstrates understanding of that work.	**Understand** that by using a structured process we can work together to better understand a longer work of fiction or nonfiction.	**Do**—share the responsibility of discussing a longer work of fiction or nonfiction, creating a project that demonstrates understanding of that work (*see MO below*).

Measurable Objective 1				
Introduction	**Thinking Verb(s)**	**Product**	**Response Criterion**	**Content**
Students will…	interpret, summarize, execute, organize	to complete structured discussion templates	that are sufficient and accurate	on a longer work of fiction or nonfiction.

Measurable Objective 2				
Introduction	**Thinking Verb(s)**	**Product**	**Response Criterion**	**Content**
Students will…	organize, attribute, execute, generate, create explain	to complete a project	that sufficiently and accurately shares	information about a longer work of fiction or nonfiction.

Differentiation		
Readiness—reading materials assigned based on reading levels	**Interests**— students choose their books and how to share them with the class	**Style**—mastery, verbal/linguistic, artistic, visual, auditory, tactual, kinesthetic

Procedures

Materials

1. Baskets or boxes of books organized by reading levels that represent the racial and gender diversity in the class. These books can be fiction or nonfiction. The baskets or boxes must have at least five different titles and enough copies for each member of the group. There should be no evidence that suggests reading levels of these baskets or boxes.

2. A copy of a practice selection or a textbook that has the selection in it.

3. Sets of "Literature Circles" role sheets. Teachers can copy or download these sheets by going to Google and typing "Literature Circles."

4. Materials for creative book projects (including poster board, markers, computers, and costumes).

Day 1

Step 1: Access students' reading levels or conduct a preassessment to determine students' reading levels (lexile or other). (This aspect of assessment also fits into Part 1 of the differentiated assessment process.)

Step 2: Group students by that reading level. Hopefully students will cluster evenly in groups of at least three. If one or two students score far below or above others, allow them to be partners or individualize if there is just one student at a certain level.

Step 3: Determine the groups based on reading levels, and then find fiction and nonfiction books that match those reading levels and the diversity of students.

Day 2

Step 1: Have the group lists on the board and desks arranged to accommodate those groups. Label the tables so that students can easily find their assigned seats.

Step 2: Tell students they are going to be participating in a "Book Study Group" with the other students in their group. Tell them that they are going to choose a book to read together, but before they do that, they need to practice how to talk about the book together.

Step 3: Tell students they are going to read a selection together, and then they will practice how each role should function when they get into their groups.

Step 4: Hand out the selection or tell students what pages to read in their textbooks. Students should read this selection silently.

Step 5: Hand out a role, such as "Discussion Leader." The role sheet should be scripted so that students know how the "Discussion Leader" should interact with the rest of the group.

Step 6: Walk students through the process of completing the role by using "Seven Hands Raised" (Smith, 2004) or some other method of interactive conversation with the class. Determine that all students have successfully completed a Discussion Leader template. Spot check by circulating around the room, and remind students that you will collect these role sheets to assure that all students have completed the form sufficiently and accurately.

Step 7: Ask students to work in their groups to complete another role sheet, such as the "Illustrator." At this point circulate and coach students through the process. Begin a gradual release of responsibility at this point, or continue to structure the completing of the form.

Step 8: Facilitate or directly instruct students as they practice completing at least two more roles.

Step 9: Collect all written work to evaluate at it and offer students feedback.

Day 3

Step 1: Review the role sheets and the process of working together to understand a book that the students will now choose to read. Make sure you have created a basket or box of fiction or nonfiction books for each of the major reading levels in the class.

Step 2: Tell students to examine the books as you circulate to coach them as they select a book together. If you have read any or all of the books, you might share your ideas about them if students seem interested in your perspective.

Step 3: When the students have selected their group's book, they should divide it into 8 reading assignment. For example, with an 160-page book, students should read approximately 20 pages per discussion. If the book has 16 chapters students might read 2 per discussion. Let students know that they should turn in at least one role sheet per person at the end of each class. Students can read during class or for homework. Students begin reading their books.

Day 4: Students finish reading the assignment if they did not finish reading assignment 1 for homework. After students have read assignment 1, they should each complete a role during their group discussion of the part of the book they read. Students should turn in their work and begin reading the next assignment.

Days 5–11:   Students read and complete role sheets.

Days 12–15:   Students decide how they will share their book with the class. Teachers might have poster board, costumes, computers, and other materials that students might use to share their books with the class. Teachers may suggest one of many types of artistic projects including the following:

- Advertisement of the book

- Skit (people or puppets) about the book

- PowerPoint presentation about the book

- Talk show or radio show about the book

Teachers can allow students class time to complete their work or students might want to work at home. On the 15th day, students should present their projects to the class. The teacher might use the project rubric in Chapter 4.

Summative Assessment Choices

- Teachers might use a standardized measure of student achievement that matches state or district standards

- Teachers might level the assessment as a means of vertically articulating curriculum standards for future grade level requirements. For example if students will need higher skill levels for advanced classes, the teacher might inspire students at any mastery level to exceed grade level standards.

- Teachers might assign students to complete an individual writing assignment about the book.

Social Studies:
Native South American Cultures Curriculum

Some students will need a great deal of structure to be able to successfully investigate a topic. Teachers might use the "Big 6" process for research. See Chapter 5 for ways to structure the following assignment (Figure 6.4, p. 184) for students who need help conducting research.

Figure 6.4. Social Studies: Native South American Cultures

Curriculum				
SCOS	**EQ:** What distinguishes South American indigenous cultures and why should we learn about them?	**Know**—important information about indigenous South American cultures, how to find and gather information, how to cite sources, how to complete a project based on multiple intelligences (knowledge will be specific to the project the student chooses).	**Understand** that it is important to learn about South America's indigenous people so that we might be better world citizens and preservers of diverse cultures.	**Do**—choose an indigenous South American culture listed below, or find one of your own. Learn about them and draw conclusions about why we should learn about them (*see MO below*).

Measurable Objective				
Introduction	**Thinking Verb(s)**	**Product**	**Response Criterion**	**Content**
Students will…	recall, organize, classify, interpret, explain, generate, create, plan, and produce	a multiple intelligence product	evaluated using criterion from the rubric	for an indigenous culture in South America.

Differentiation		
Readiness—students choose topics, sources of information, and level of mastery	**Interests**—multiple intelligences project matrix; students choose topics based on their interests	**Style**—mastery, multiple intelligence choices

Procedures

Teachers should direct students to use the online or hard copy sources of information about at least three ancient ethnic groups from South America (or other continent). Teachers can use other indigenous groups, but these three have lots of information about them. Encourage students to explore these cultures and to choose one of the projects listed here as project assessments of their learning. *Teachers should emphasize that students should include in their work an explanation of why we might want to learn about these cultures.*

Intelligence	Products
Verbal/Linguistic	Students will write a five-page report citing at least five sources on the Yagua, Arawak, or Aymara.
Mathematical	Students will collect data about the Yagua, Arawak, or Aymara to create a graphical representation with 3-page commentary. Students must cite at least 5 sources.
Musical	Students will create a photo story set to music that includes at least 15 slides that show information about the Yagua, Arawak, or Aymara. Students must cite at least five sources.
Kinesthetic	Students will create a movement or act out (with people or puppets) a skit (must be at least five written pages) that provides information about the Yagua, Arawak, or Aymara. The movement must have a three-page commentary. Students must cite at least five sources.
Spatial	Students will create a piece of art that is representative of the Yagua, Arawak, or Aymara. Students must write a two-page commentary and cite at least five sources.

Students will present their products during class. Each student will have 5 minutes to make his or her presentation. Figure 6.5 is a rubric to address the evaluation of each of these product choices including the presentation to the class. After the presentation the class will go into "workshop mode" during which the teacher and other students will act as coaches and consultants

Figure 6.5. Rubric for Multiple Intelligences Product

Categories	1	2	3	4
Sufficiency	Project falls short of the content required by the project description. Information includes mostly common knowledge. The student does not include sufficient sources for the project.	Project falls short of the content required by the project description. Information includes common knowledge and lacks strong evidence of differentiating for importance. The student includes sufficient sources.	Project includes the correct content required by the project description. Information shows evidence of differentiating for importance. The student includes the required number of sources.	Project exceeds (but is not excessive) the content required by the project description. Information is complex and detailed. The student includes more than the required number of sources.
Accuracy	The product has several errors, and the student does not draw conclusions about the facts.	There are some flaws in the information and/or in the conclusions the student draws about it.	All information is accurate and important to know. Student draws conclusions that are logical about the topic.	All information is accurate and important to know. Student synthesizes facts to draw important conclusions about the topic.
Presentation	Student uses much less time than allotted, fidgets, says "um" often, laughs inappropriately, and does not use props or other materials effectively.	Student exceeds or uses less time than allotted, fidgets, says "um" often, and does not use props or materials effectively.	Student adheres to the time limit, makes appropriate eye contact, speaks effectively, and uses props or other materials to make the presentation.	Student closely adheres to time limit, maintains a charismatic relationship with the audience, voice level is appropriate, and effectively uses props or other materials to make the presentation.

Summative Assessment

♦ Teachers can assess students based on standardized achievement goals that respond to district or state expectations.

♦ Teachers can use students' presentations as summative.

English/Social Studies—Virtual Library Project

Teachers might use the following unit (Figure 6.6) as a simulation or as a real purchasing event if either the social studies or English teachers have some money with which to buy new books for a personal or school library. This short unit has wonderful results especially if the teacher can actually purchase the books.

Figure 6.6. English/Social Studies—Virtual Library

Curriculum				
SCOS	**EQ:** What books do we want to read (or buy for our class or school)?	**Know**—how to examine books without going to a library, how to write a 1-minute speech persuading peers to choose a book.	**Understand** that it is possible to choose a good book without going to a library.	**Do**—choose a book, explore the book using online sources, and write a 1-minute persuasive speech to "pitch the book" to peers (*see MO below*).

Measurable Objective				
Introduction	**Thinking Verb(s)**	**Product**	**Response Criterion**	**Content**
Students will…	explain, generate, create, plan, and produce	a 1-minute speech	that persuades peers to read (or purchase)	a book about Russia.

Differentiation		
Readiness—students choose books on their grade level	**Interests**—students choose books of interest to them	**Style**—mastery, verbal/linguistic, interpersonal, self-expressive

Procedures

Day 1

Step 1: Tell students that they are going to identify books that the class might read (or that the teacher or librarian might buy for the class or school library).

Step 2: Identify a website that has book titles with lexile levels, grade levels, and categories. For example if the teacher is a social studies teacher, he or she might want to find some books on Russia that might be of interest to sixth-grade students. Teachers can use the website, http://www.flr. follett.com/login, to access titles of books by reading levels on the topic of Russia. Students and teachers might also go to www.lexiles.com to find the lexile level for any book they identify. Teachers will help students understand how to interpret lexiles and will make sure students have some idea of what their lexile reading level is.

Step 3: Ask students to identify a book title or several that they want to investigate.

Step 4: Ask students to go the www.Amazon.com to look for these books so that they can see what the cover looks like, the publishers information, and what reviewers say about the book. Through this process students identify a book they want to "pitch to the class."

Day 2

Step 1: As homework or class work, students write a 1-minute speech "pitching their book" on an index card.

Step 2: Students make their speeches one by one. They put their cards on the board with the title of their book clearly visible.

Step 3: Three or four at time, students go to the board to vote on a number of books. Say, "We need to choose five books, so vote for five." Votes might be signified by stickers or check marks on the cards. Tally the votes and announce the winners on Day 3.

Summary

In this chapter, teachers have seen how to use various types of assessment together to teach a unit of study. Unless they have a highly specialized roster, most secondary teachers face a wide variety of student needs. It is critical that teachers learn as much as they can about how to meet their students where they are to facilitate their movement toward learning.

References

Alderman, M. (1990). Motivation for at-risk students. *Educational Leadership, 48,* 27–30.

Allen, R. (2007). *TrainSmart: Effective training every time.* Thousand Oaks, CA: Corwin Press.

Anderson, L., Krathwohl, D., Airasian, P., Cruikshank, K., Mayer, R., Pintrich, P., Raths, J., & Wittrock, M. (Eds.). (2001). *A taxonomy for learning, teaching, and assessing: A revision of Bloom's taxonomy of educational objectives.* New York: Longman.

Aronson, E., Blaney, N., Stephan, C., Sikes, J., & Snapp, M. (1978). *The jigsaw classroom.* Beverly Hills, CA: Sage.

Ausubel, D. (1963). *The psychology of meaningful verbal learning,* New York: Grune & Stratton.

Ausubel, D. (1968). *Educational psychology, a cognitive view.* New York: Holt, Rinehart, & Winston.

Belvel, P., & Jordan, M. (2003). *Rethinking classroom management: Strategies for prevention, intervention, and problem solving.* Thousand Oaks, CA: Corwin Press.

Bruner, J. (1973). *Beyond the information given: Studies in the psychology of learning.* Oxford: W. W. Norton.

Butler, K. (1984). *Learning and teaching styles in theory and practice.* Columbia, CT: Learner's Dimension.

Butler, K. (1987). Successful learning strategies for the emerging adolescent. *Oklahoma Middle Level Education Association Journal,* 1–7.

Daniels, H. (1994). *Literature circles: Voice and choice in the student centered classroom.* Portland, ME: Stenhouse Publishers.

DeVries, D., Edwards, K., & Slavin, R. (1978). Biracial learning teams and race relations in the classroom: Four field experiments using teams-games-tournaments. *Journal of Educational Psychology, 70(3),* 356–362.

Dunn, R., & Dunn, K. (1993). *Teaching secondary students through their individual learning styles: Practical approaches for grades 7–12.* Boston, MA: Allyn and Bacon.

Erikson, E. (1950). *Childhood and society.* New York: W. W. Norton.

Fisher, D., & Frey, N. (2007). *Checking for understanding: Formative assessment techniques for your classroom.* Alexandria, VA: Association for Supervision and Curriculum Development.

Gardner, H. (1993). *Multiple intelligences: The theory in practice.* New York: Basic Books.

Gick, M., & Holyoak, K. (1980). Analogical problem solving. *Cognitive Psychology, 12,* 306–355.

Gordon, W. (1961). *Synectices: The development of creative capacity.* New York: Harper.

Ginn, W. (2003). *Jean Piaget—Intellectual Development.* Accessed September 20, 2003 at http://www.sk.com.br/sk-piage.html.

Herber, H. (1978). *Teaching reading in the content areas.* Englewood Cliffs, NJ: Prentice Hall.

Hunter, R. (2004). *Madeline Hunter's mastery teaching: Increasing instructional effectiveness in elementary and secondary schools* (updated edition). Thousand Oaks, CA: Corwin Press.

Jensen, E. (1998). *Teaching with the brain in mind.* Alexandria, VA: Association for Supervision and Curriculum Development.

Jones, V., & Jones, L. (1990). *Comprehensive classroom management: Motivating and managing students* (3rd ed.). Boston, MA: Allyn and Bacon.

Kagen, S. (1997). *Cooperative learning.* San Clemente, CA: Kagan Professional Development.

Keene, E., & Zimmerman, S. (1997). *Mosaic of thought: Teaching comprehension in a reader's workshop.* Portsmouth, NH: Heinemann.

Marzano, R. (2004). *Building background knowledge for academic achievement: Research on what works in schools.* Alexandria, VA: Association for Supervision and Curriculum Development.

Marzano, R., Pickering, D., & Pollock, J. (2001). *Classroom instruction that works: Research-based strategies for increasing student achievement.* Alexandria, VA: Association for Supervision and Curriculum Development.

Mosston, M. (1972). *Teaching: From command to discovery.* Belmont, CA: Wadsworth Publishing.

Northey, S. (2005). *Handbook on differentiating instruction in middle and high school.* Larchmont, NY: Eye on Education.

O'Brien, L. (1990). *Learning channels; Preference checklist.* Philadelphia, PA: Research for Better Schools.

Ogle, D. (1986). A teaching model that develops active reading of expository text. *The Reading Teacher, 39*(6), 564–570.

Opitz, M., & Rasinski, T. (1998). *Good-bye round robin: 25 effective oral reading strategies.* Portsmouth, NH: Heinemann.

Ray, K. (1999). *Wondrous words: Writers and writing in the elementary classroom.* Urbana, IL: National Council of Teachers of English.

Resnick, L. (2000). Making America smarter. *Education Week, 18(40),* 38-40.

Rief, L. (1998). *Vision and voice: Expanding the literacy spectrum.* Portsmouth, NH: Heinemann.

Sagor, R., & Cox, J. (2004). *At-risk students: Reaching and teaching them* (2nd ed.). Larchmont, NY: Eye on Education.

Schoenbach, R., Greenleaf, C., Cziko, C., & Hurwitz, L. (1999). *Reading for understanding: A guide to improving reading in middle and high school classrooms: The reading apprenticeship guidebook.* San Francisco, CA: Jossey-Bass.

Silver, H., & Strong, R. (2004). *Learning style inventory for students.* Ho-Ho-Kus, NJ: Thoughtful Education Press.

Silver, H., Strong, W., & Perini, M. (2007). *The strategic teacher: Selecting the right research-based strategy for every lesson.* Alexandria, VA: Association for Supervision and Curriculum Development.

Smith, R. (2004). *Conscious classroom management: Unlocking the secrets of great teaching.* San Rafael, CA: Conscious Teaching Publications.

Sternberg, R. (1997). *Thinking styles.* New York: Cambridge University Press.

Stiggins, R., Arter, J., Chappuis, J., & Chappuis, S. (2007). *Classroom assessment for student learning: Doing it right-using it well.* Upper Saddle River, NJ: Merrill/Prentice Hall.

Strong, R., Hanson, J., & Silver, H. (1995). *Questioning styles and strategies* (3rd ed.). Woodbridge, NJ: Thoughtful Education Press.

Strong, R., Silver, H., Perini, M., & Tuculescu, G. (2002). *Reading for academic success: Powerful strategies for struggling average and advanced readers, grades 7–12.* Thousand Oaks, CA: Corwin Press.

Suchman, J. (1966). *Developing inquiry.* Chicago: Science Research Associates.

Taba, H. (1971). *Hilda Taba teaching strategies program.* Miami, FL: Institute for Staff Development.

Tomlinson, C. (1995). *How to differentiate instruction in mixed-ability classrooms.* Alexandria, VA: Association for Supervision and Curriculum Development.

Tomlinson, C. (1999). *The differentiated classroom: Responding to the needs of all learners.* Alexandria, VA: Association for Supervision and Curriculum Development.

Tomlinson, C. (2003). *Differentiation in practice: A resource guide for differentiating curriculum, grades 5–9.* Alexandria, VA: Association for Supervision and Curriculum Development.

Tovani, C. (2000). *I read it, but I don't get it: Comprehension strategies for adolescent readers.* Portland, Me: Stenhouse Publishers.

Trussell-Cullen, A. (1998). *Assessment: In the learner-centered classroom.* Carlsbad, CA: Dominie Press.

Vygotsky, L. (1978). Interaction between learning and development. In M. Cole, V. John-Steiner, S. Scribner, & E. Souberman, (Eds.), *Mind in society: The development of higher psychological process* (pp. 79–92). Cambridge, MA: Harvard University Press.

Waterman, S. (2007). *The democratic differentiated classroom.* Larchmont, NY: Eye on Education.

Weiner, B. (1985). An attributional theory of motivation and emotion. *Psychological Review, 92,* 548–573.

Wiggins, G., & McTighe, J. (1998). *Understanding by design.* Alexandria, VA: Association for Supervision and Curriculum Development.

Wormeli, R. (2006). *Fair isn't always equal; Assessing & grading in the differentiated classroom.* Portland, ME: Stenhouse Publishers.

Wood, K. (2001). *Strategies for integrating reading and writing.* Winterville, OH: National Middle School Association.

Wu, B. (1999). *The Internet, computer games, and morality; Ethics, technology, and science.* Accessed from ThinkQuest.org April 18, 2008 at http://www.thinkquest.org/ 29435/morality/index.html.